EXTENDED
Horizon Reflections

EXTENDED
Horizon Reflections

My Story and What I've Learned about Life
and Identity along the Way

JEFF JACKSON

Charleston, SC
www.PalmettoPublishing.com

Extended Horizon Reflections

Copyright © 2021 by Jeff Jackson

All rights reserved

First Edition

Hardcover ISBN: 978-1-63837-263-9
Paperback ISBN: 978-1-63837-264-6
eBook ISBN: 978-1-63837-265-3

CONTENTS

PREFACE

I've loved to write since I learned how to read. I was the weird kid in elementary school who actually enjoyed writing about what I did over the summer or what our family did on our vacation. In high school, I was the nerd who chose to take the creative-writing class as an elective rather than wood, metal, or auto shop. That was the time my journaling habit began, and it has continued on a sporadic, but fairly regular basis, up until today. In addition to journaling, I've also written more than one hundred family and personal newsletters, blog posts, and over a dozen articles for a couple of different magazines. And it's probably no surprise that someone who likes to write as much as I do also enjoys writing poetry. I'll grant you that it's not very good poetry, but poetry nonetheless.

I always thought my first book would be a novel, but because so many of my family members and friends have told me that they think my life story is more unique and more interesting than their own and most people that they know, I took their advice to make my own life story the priority. The fact that I've been a pack rat with my journaling over the years minimized the challenge of recalling the details of my story and how I felt at the time each incident in my life took place. And although I didn't begin with a plan to include any of my own poems, I concluded that to give you as clear a picture as possible of who I am, I needed to include a few of them in my story at the points on my timeline when I wrote them.

It's probably not surprising that I've chosen the common method of telling my story in chronological order and in the way things unfolded. What may differ is the way I've broken it up into chapters using the most significant identity labels I've acquired along the way. My current understanding and convictions about who I am in my own eyes, in the eyes of others, and especially in the eyes of God, seemed like a reasonable and fairly unique way to let myself be known. I hope you'll agree.

CHAPTER ONE

Son, Family Member, Teammate (1958–1974)

A family in nonstop motion

I'm not sure how many times I heard my mom and dad tell the story of how we made the move to California, but I loved listening to it every time they did. Whenever someone would ask if we were originally from California, one of them would reply that we were from Denver and launch into the tale of our journey to the Golden State. My dad would begin telling the story by naming the Chevy dealership in Denver where he was working during the first few months of 1963. He'd then paint a vivid word picture of a particularly blustery day in February. According to him, a snowstorm had just blanketed the city with enough snow to require even the most seasoned natives of the area to string snow chains around their car tires. After the storm had passed, the snow accumulated, and the temperature dropped to just above zero degrees. At that time of the year, it was still dark out when he would leave the house every morning at dawn to go to work.

On that fateful day, he stepped out of the house and into the icy, predawn morning air to leave for work. He recalled his cheeks freezing and his nose running during the mere thirty-foot trek from the house to the car. It was then that he noticed his rear tire on the driver's side had gone flat, and instantly his temper flared. It was always at this point of telling his story that my mom would begin nodding in agreement with his highly animated, detailed reenactment of the anger that steamed out of him that morning. He resumed the story, recalling how many times he had to shuffle back and forth to the house to warm up in between jacking up the car, taking off the chains, removing the tire, putting the spare on, and then finally putting the snow chains back on. It had taken him about a half hour to finish what would have otherwise been a menial task for him, and his anger intensified when he realized that he was going to be late for work.

He would be really wound up by this point in the story and then give the clincher. He said that when the car was finally ready, he had gone back into the house one last time to give Mom a kiss goodbye. It was in that very moment that he made the life-altering decision—he said to her, "Beverly, we're moving to California!" Mom would always chime in on this part and say, "And I said to him 'When do you want to leave?'" The two of them would then trade off giving the details of what transpired over the next few months after they made the decision to make the move. And as crazy as it sounds, a few months later, that's exactly what they did. In June of 1963, three months before I turned five years old, they loaded my older brother, Rick, and me, along with a few belongings, into their 1953 Ford and followed Route 66 all the way to Southern California. And they never looked back.

The road trip ended in Santa Monica, where we moved into an apartment near the beach. My dad was a skilled mechanic, so he found work in another Chevy dealership within a few days of our arrival. The prospect of never having to deal with ice, snow, or freezing temperatures again excited both of them tremendously. That, coupled with the never-ending auto repair needs of a few million people living in a car-heavy culture, catapulted the possibility of ever leaving Southern California completely from their minds.

Due to his aforementioned skills as a mechanic and his quick temper, my dad changed jobs regularly. He never had to work for a boss he didn't like for too long because there was always another local dealership that was on the lookout for mechanics who knew what they were doing. It also meant that we moved to a new apartment or rental house in different cities on a consistent basis. Less than a year after we arrived in Santa Monica, we moved to Burbank, then to West Hollywood, and then an hour or so North, to Lancaster in the high desert. We relocated so often that I attended eight different elementary schools before I finished the fourth grade. It didn't just seem like I was always the new kid in class; I really was. My main experience as an elementary school student consisted of continuously accepting and adjusting to new surroundings, an experience most of my classmates couldn't relate to. Fortunately, I was a resilient child, and the changes didn't really bother me.

Even though my dad was the primary breadwinner in our family, the higher cost of living in Southern California required my mom to begin working outside of the home. My earliest memory of her having a job was when I was in the second or third grade, when we were living in the Los Angeles area. I have vivid memories of her workplace, an old-fashioned drugstore with a soda fountain at the front of the store. In addition to selling sandwiches and other food items, there were all kinds of sweet treats, including ice cream. My brother and I would stop by there on our walks home from school, and more often than not, she would have us sit right up to the counter and then whip us up delicious chocolate malt shakes. Later, during our two years in Lancaster, she took a part-time job as a bank teller, and that became her career until she retired at the age of sixty-five.

Family name label, awareness awakened

While living there, my parents signed my brother and me up to play Little League baseball. What I came to experience on the first day of practice of my first season planted a seed that I knew was significant at the time but that would take many years to grow and even more years for me to fully understand.

My dad had just brought me to the field and as I was milling around with the other kids, a man with a dark-blue windbreaker and cap approached us. There was a jam-packed duffel bag hanging off of one shoulder and a clipboard in one of his hands. He dropped the duffel bag to the ground, called all of us over to him, introduced himself, and told us how proud he was to be the head coach of the Hawks and how happy he was that each of us were on his team. Then, he looked down at his clipboard and told us to say "Here" when he called each of our names.

I really wasn't paying attention as he went through the roster alphabetically by our last names, and when he got to my name on the list, he just called out "Jackson." I didn't hear Jeffrey or Jeff, so I didn't respond immediately. I was expecting him to use my first name like my teachers always did, but he didn't. And because I hesitated, he called out my last name again, so I shot my hand up as quickly as I could and said, "Here."

Hearing my last name called out that second time triggered a good feeling within me, one that I had never experienced prior to that moment. I didn't know why it felt good; I just knew that it did. And that good feeling lasted the whole season, becoming ignited each and every time my coaches, other players, and parents referred to me as "Jackson." And although it wasn't the same level of pleasure I felt by hearing the name Jackson out loud, I experienced a similar feeling every time I wore my team hat and T-shirt with my number on the back: confident and pleased by the fact that others were acknowledging me as a member of my team.

It took me a few years, and a few more seasons of being on sports teams, to find a way to describe what being identified as part of a group that was distinct from other groups felt like, but eventually I did. It was like I had an itch within me to be identified by others as part of a group, but I didn't know it was there until it was scratched. I equate it to the unique feeling of pleasure all of us have experienced when someone starts rubbing and then scratching our back. That hard-to explain feeling of pleasure and satisfaction that is stimulated when someone scratches our back and we become aware of an itch we didn't know we had, but was already there, waiting and wanting to be given some attention.

A promise to stay put for a while

My mom never did like the dry heat, air, and wind that was part of life in the high desert, so my dad began looking for work back down in the parts of Southern California that weren't far from the beach. He eventually landed a job at a dealership in La Jolla, and she was more than thrilled to pack up and make the move to the San Diego area. When we loaded up the U-Haul to make the long drive down the old Highway 395, we had spent a little more than two years in Lancaster, and I had gone to two different elementary schools. We moved into an apartment in the Clairemont area of San Diego in early 1969, and I finished up my fifth-grade year at an elementary school near where we lived. We moved a few miles west over the summer break, which required changing schools, and I was the new kid at a new school once again. Even though we did make another move from one house to another during my sixth-grade year, we stayed within the same school district, and I was able to complete the whole year at the same school.

While living in San Diego, our parents signed up my brother and me to play Little League baseball again. We told them we loved to play football too, so after baseball season ended, they signed us up to play Pop Warner football. Due to the nature of football, and the reality that not only age but weight also mattered, there were minimums and maximums for each in order to be allowed to play. At the time we started the practices, I weighed in under the minimum weight limit of sixty-five pounds. I wound up eating peanut butter and banana sandwiches, and other high-calorie foods, to gain enough to play. I eventually made the weight, but was still so small and fearful of getting hurt that I really didn't do well that first year.

Just as in the baseball teams, the football coaches also referred to us by our last names. So, every time I played organized sports, I was called Jackson and wore the gear I was given by each team that declared I was a member, and I experienced the pleasure of having that "group-identity" itch scratched once again.

About a month after I finished the sixth grade, in early July of 1970, my dad took a job at a dealership in the city of Escondido, about twenty miles north of where we had been living. I wasn't aware of it at the time, but before agreeing to make the move there, my mom had a talk with my dad. She told him that if we went, we would need to remain in place there until my brother and I finished high school. My dad agreed and said that if he needed to find work later on, he would limit his job hunt to within the greater San Diego area, and if he landed a job, he would make the commute back and forth.

Within weeks of arriving in Escondido in the summer of 1970, we began playing Pop Warner football, and the Tuesday after Labor Day, I started seventh grade at Grant Junior High School. I had made a few friends on the football team who were also my classmates at the new school, but I followed the pattern I'd developed of proceeding slowly in really getting to know them, for fear we would probably move again sometime soon. At the time, because I was unaware that my parents had decided to stay in the same place until we finished high school, I did what I was prone to do at a new school: focusing my attention on the subjects I was supposed to be learning.

The time passed quickly, and I did well in my studies. By the end of the year, I had a small group of friends whom I became very close with. Even though we moved from one apartment complex to another during that first year, and then into a house at the beginning of my eighth-grade year, I was more than happy that I had been able to go to the same school for two years and graduate from junior high with all the same friends I had come to know while I was there. A few weeks before starting ninth grade in 1972, our parents finally assured my brother and me that we could count on graduating from Escondido High School four years later, and they were true to their word.

My freshmen year went well. I had really begun to enjoy reading in junior high school, and that pleasure continued. But I also began to enjoy writing, and by the end of the school year, I decided that I either wanted to become a sports broadcaster or a journalist. I used my elective classes in my sophomore and junior years to take creative-writing classes and journalism rather than auto, metal, or wood shop like most of my friends. I knew that I probably needed to go to college to pursue either of those professions. But I also knew that our family didn't have the funds to pay for me to go, so I pretty much put those thoughts on the back burner of my mind.

Out of escrow and into a gift from God

Not long after Christmas break of my sophomore year, my parents tried to buy a house for the first time since we lived in Lancaster. Their attempt failed when the house fell out of escrow for some unforeseen reason. With home ownership no longer a possibility, we had to relocate once again, this time to an apartment complex less than a mile away from the small house we had been renting. We had no idea at the time, but moving into that apartment complex in early 1974 would change the trajectory of two families—ours and that of a single mom and her three daughters who were already living there when we arrived.

CHAPTER TWO

Boyfriend, Enlistee, Graduate (1974–1976)

Love at first sight

My brother and I were on our high school swimming team at the time, and we were excited about living in an apartment complex that had a pool. Even though we spent a few hours each day in the YMCA pool at practice for the team, we began frequenting the one at our complex at night and on the weekends. A few weeks after we moved in, I meandered out there to check out what was happening. It was a sunny Saturday afternoon, and I peered through the wrought-iron fence to see if I knew any of the people that were there. A family with a couple of young kids were down near the shallow end of the pool, but what drew my attention was a small group of three girls, right around my age, in bikinis. They were lying on their towels not far from the edge of the deep end. This was the first time I had ever seen them there.

I was a typical fifteen-year-old boy, so as soon as I opened and walked through the gate, I zeroed in on them to get a clearer picture of what these girls actually looked like. One of them was blond, and the other two were brunettes. Even though it was clear they were all there trying to start or increase their tans for the summer that was just a few months away, my eyes were drawn to the girl with the dark, wavy hair, who had much darker skin than the other two and filled out her lime-green bikini very nicely. I threw my towel down on a lounge chair that was positioned just right for me to continue gawking at the most beautiful girl I had ever seen, when something ignited inside of me.

I literally could not take my eyes off of her, and as crazy as it sounds, I knew at that very moment that she was going to be my girlfriend soon, and hopefully my wife at some later point in time. I know the whole "love at first sight" thing sounds like something from a fairy tale, but if it wasn't an actual experience for some people—and a desire of many others—the possibility of something like that actually happening wouldn't reso-nate with as many folks as it does, myself included.

All I can say is that for me, at the age of fifteen, in my sophomore year of high school, the first time I saw this girl I fell in love with her, and every fiber of my being longed to spend the rest of my life with her. I hadn't met her yet, had never heard her voice, and didn't know her name, but I knew she was the one. I never approached the three of them that afternoon. I just tried to look cool and keep my eye on them, particularly the one in the green bikini. Eventually, the three of them sat up on their beach towels, and I could see her mannerisms as she interacted with the other two. She glanced in my direction a few times, but it didn't seem like anything special about me registered with her.

After about an hour, I went back to our apartment and continued on with whatever I had to do the rest of that day—but I couldn't get this girl out of my mind, or my heart. As I went to bed that night, I began crying out to God in prayer with an intensity level that I had always longed for but was never able to attain. I begged Him to give me the opportunity to meet her as soon as possible, and I began asking Him that night to somehow make it possible for the two of us to be married at some future point in time.

A few days later, after repeating that prayer each night before falling asleep, I met the blond girl out near the pool. I struck up a conversation with her and learned that her name was Marie and that she was fourteen. I asked her who the dark, wavy-haired girl in the green bikini was, and she said it was her sister, Helen, who was thirteen. I don't really remember how the rest of the conversation went; all I knew was that I finally knew the name of the girl I was in love with and longed to have as my wife someday. Next, all I needed to do was actually *meet* the girl of my dreams and win her over.

Eventually, her sister introduced us, and I finally spoke to Helen for the first time. The sound of her voice and her gentle, humble demeanor amplified what I was already feeling for her. She was going to the same junior high that I had gone to, and even though I wanted to spend every waking moment with her, my schooling and commitments as a swim team member and the part-time job I had put a major crimp in my ability to do that. But even with the minimal amount of time I was able to spend with her those first few months, I decided to ask her to go steady with me.

While I was in that process of getting to know Helen, my brother, Rick, had become very interested in her blond-haired sister, Marie, whom I had originally talked with. Because he already had his driver's license and his own car—a very cool 1955 two-door Chevy wagon—we would go out and about with the two of them in the front seat and Helen and me sitting in the back. And it's probably no surprise that Helen and Marie's friends were as intrigued as ours were when they discovered that brothers were dating sisters.

Becoming a boyfriend and avoiding consequences

On June 8, 1974, standing out on the sidewalk in front of her apartment just before she went in for the night, I held out a metal cross on a necklace I had bought just for the purpose and asked her to go steady with me. I was really nervous. My voice didn't have its regular confidence or volume, and my hands were shaking a little bit, but I had mustered the courage to do what I knew I needed to do. I'll never forget the way her eyes immediately watered up and the look on her face as she said, "Yes." Deep in my heart of hearts, I had hoped that her acceptance of that very basic, but meaningful, expression of our commitment to focus our romantic feelings only on one another, as important as it was, would be the first step of our lifetime journey together.

I went home that night and thanked God with a greater passion than I ever had before, and intensified my pleading with Him to move things along toward my end goal of eventually marrying the fairest of maidens who had chosen to become my steady girlfriend. When I told my brother and friends the next day and she told her sisters and girlfriends, being acknowledged by others as her boyfriend provoked that same feeling I had that first day of Little League practice so many years before. A previously unknown itch to be identified and labeled as Helen's boyfriend, rather than just being viewed as an average teenaged boy, was incredibly soothing and satisfying to my soul.

Although I was sure there were a million other fifteen-year-old boys going steady with their thirteen-year-old girlfriends around our country, I was prideful enough to think that our connection and loyalty to one another was different. I was also mistakenly convinced that we were almost at the commitment level of being engaged, as both a private and public declaration of our plans to get married at some point in the near future and grow old together. I know that having those kinds of thoughts at that age sounded completely crazy, or incredibly naïve (or both), but that is how I viewed what began that night.

With that view of our relationship, the natural inclinations of a teenage boy with a beautiful girlfriend he was genuinely convinced he was going to marry at some point in the future, along with the sexual morality of the culture of the midseventies—well, I don't believe I need to provide any detail about the depth of our connection with each other that took place by the time we celebrated our sixth month of going steady. In order to ensure that we could continue to enjoy this level of pleasure while minimizing the possibility of experiencing the natural consequences, we went to a nearby government-sponsored organization to obtain the pills that helped us achieve that goal—without the knowledge or consent of our parents.

When she began attending my high school, we spent an enormous amount of time together and loved every minute of it. I was keeping a journal at the time, and the assignments for my creative-writing class fanned the flames of my desire to begin writing short poems for her. I probably wrote a half of a dozen or so during our first year of going steady. The only one that we still have today is this poem that I printed on the back of my senior picture that I gave to her in January of 1976:

> These 19 months that I've been with you
> Have proved to me that "true love" is true
>
> For when I am down and needing a lift,
> You're always right there with your special gift
>
> To write why I love you would take me a year,
> And even then, it wouldn't be clear
>
> So I write you this poem with love on my mind,
> Knowing we'll stay together, whatever we find
>
> I love you,
> Jeff

Lunch at McDonald's and marching toward the military

In the midst of spending every possible moment with Helen, I was constantly thinking about how to best pursue the decision I had made to become a sports broadcaster or a journalist. Even though I had no idea where the money would come from for me to attend college in order to accomplish that goal, I went ahead and took the SAT and applied to San Diego State University. This made sense to me because it would keep me somewhat local, and Helen and I could continue our journey together toward marriage. But I was beginning to sense a conflict going on within me. As much as I loved Helen and my family, a part of me had grown to love, and look back fondly on, the feeling I had each time we moved. It was another of those quirky things about me that I couldn't explain, but there was something about being disconnected from the familiar and comfortable and plunged into a new and different context that exhilarated me. I kept these thoughts to myself, but they definitely contributed to what happened next and how things have unfolded in my life since.

At the beginning of the second semester of my senior year of high school, I received an acceptance letter to attend San Diego State University. A few weeks after the letter arrived, I bumped into one of my fellow seniors while I was grabbing lunch off campus at McDonald's. This guy was much smarter than I was. He had significantly higher grades, and his SAT score was in the top 10 percent of the whole country, which meant that he probably could have gone to any college that he wanted to.

He was already eating his meal when I sat down across the table from him and began digging into mine. I asked him which university he would be attending in the fall, and to my complete surprise, he said that he wasn't going to college—yet. He told me that he had decided to join the army instead. I was stunned. I couldn't believe this guy would choose to join the army and told him how surprising that decision was to me. After hearing his reasoning (some of which was obviously the opportunity that being an airborne Ranger provided for adventure, excitement, and the ability to fire a variety of weapons and legally blow things up), I had this incredible desire to join him and also do the college "thing" later on.

Without giving my parents a heads-up on what I was thinking or doing, a few days later, I paid a visit to the army recruiter's office. I told the recruiter about my situation and my conversation with my friend (that they obviously already knew took place), and then watched the videos of airborne Rangers. They had the bait and knew how to package and toss it to me, and I bit—hook, line, and sinker. Without my parents' knowledge, I signed up to take the Armed Services Vocational Aptitude Battery (ASVAB) test and scored highly. I didn't pay attention to how many different job opportunities my score opened up to me because I was convinced that I was going to become an airborne Ranger, just like my classmate was.

Unfamiliar anger
and conflict with my parents

After I had jumped through all of the preliminary hoops that the initial intake process requires, I honestly didn't believe that one small detail, like needing my parents to sign for me because I was only seventeen years old, would be that big of a deal. I figured they would be fairly disappointed because I wasn't going to go to college. But since they'd always communicated their love and respect for those in the military, and they always said they just wanted us to be happy, I honestly didn't think that they would even hesitate to provide their signatures on my behalf. I just needed to convince them that being an airborne Ranger was what would really make me happy.

A few days later, as our normal family discussion of the day's events was taking place around the dinner table, I began the conversation by trying to describe to my parents this thing inside me that was stirring up a hunger for doing something out of the ordinary. I said that as cool as it was to be accepted to San Diego State, I just didn't think that path would satisfy what was welling up within me. I told them about the meeting at McDonald's with my friend but limited what I said to the fact that he was going into the army, not mentioning the airborne Ranger idea. I told them that I really felt that joining the army would make me happier than staying local and going to college.

Their reaction to my desire to change my plan for my immediate future was pretty much what I had expected. They weren't totally surprised, but they did express clear disappointment as they asked me how far I'd already gone down the path of enlisting. When I told them how deep into the process I had already gone, a tinge of frustration appeared on their faces. Frustration quickly morphed into shock, and then anger, after I described the noble and heroic role of an airborne Ranger, and how I believed following my buddy's footsteps into that assignment would bring me the happiness that I was seeking.

The anger they both expressed caught me totally off guard. They told me it was ignited by how far I had gone with the intake process without telling them, and that it was fanned into a flame by not giving them the opportunity to share their thoughts about what kind of job they thought would be best for me. Although they told me they were open to the idea of signing for me if they thought the job would be helpful in life after the military, they flipped my anger switch when they stated there was no way they would sign for me to join and take the path to become an airborne Ranger.

I used as much logic and emotion as I could muster with them to try to get them to see my point of view, but it was clear that they had made up their minds. I was furious with my parents at a level I'd never experienced before, and we had the most heated argument I've ever had with them. For the first time in my life, I was overtaken with the kind of anger toward my parents that many of my friends said they had toward their parents on a weekly or even daily basis. But this kind of anger toward my parents was totally foreign to me, and I didn't know what to do.

I finally stood up, walked away from the table, and headed toward the front door so I could go out for a walk and do some thinking. Before my hand reached for the doorknob, an alarm went off inside my head. I realized that I was on the verge of having a hatred toward them that was unwarranted and needed to be conquered or else my relationship with them might be damaged beyond repair. That realization wasn't enough to cause me to turn around and go talk it through with them, but it helped keep me mentally balanced as I headed out the door and meandered around the neighborhood, pondering what had just happened and what I was going to do next.

When I opened the door and walked back into the house, they were sitting in the living room watching television. I had planned on walking right by them and straight to my bedroom. But my dad stood up, turned down the television, and instructed me to sit down. This strange behavior told me that they were feeling as troubled as I was about the way the conversation had gone and what had unfolded. I plopped down on the love seat and glared at them sitting next to each other on the couch, and I had no desire to say anything to them at that moment.

Discovering a better option

My dad said that they had talked it through and that if I was sure I wanted to go into the army, they would sign for me to do so, but not for me to enter into the course to become an airborne Ranger. They told me that if I asked the recruiter to come to our house to share with the three of us the other job options available based on my scores, it would be much easier for them to give their consent. It wasn't what I wanted to hear, but I had to admit that it did make sense, and I agreed to do it.

The following week, the recruiter I had been interacting with came over to our house after dinner. My parents explained their concerns about me joining for that occupation, and he told them he understood their perspective. He went on to tell them that my Armed Services Vocational Aptitude Battery scores were higher than average, and as a result, there were close to three hundred jobs that I could select from.

After describing a wide range of vocations that were available to me, he mentioned that my scores were high enough to qualify for the tests given for entrance to the military intelligence field. He went on to explain that those specialized tests were only given at the Armed Forces Examining and Entrance Station (AFEES) station in Los Angeles, and that if I passed the tests and enlisted in one of those occupations, a very thorough background investigation would be done on me by the Department of Defense. My parents' approval for me to go to Los Angeles for those tests was clinched when he informed them that a job in that field would pretty much guarantee me a great career in government after I was discharged.

Joining Uncle Sam's family

The recruiter set everything into place, and a few weeks later, I was at the AFEES station, on Wilshire Boulevard, in Los Angeles. I was administered the strangest tests I'd ever seen, passed them (somehow), and was taken to an office in the building separate from where everything else was going on. The staff sergeant behind the desk told me I qualified to become part of a specialized unit called the Army Security Agency (ASA). He gave me an overview of what that entailed and then explained the different occupations that made it possible for them to accomplish their mission. With his help, I narrowed it down to a specific job that required six months of specialized schooling after completing basic training.

I boarded the bus back to Oceanside and handed my packet of documents over to the recruiter as I got into his car for the drive back to my house in Escondido. As soon as I walked through the door, my dad told me to turn off the television and tell them about my entire experience. They listened with intensity to every word I said, asking questions along the way, and when I finished, they asked me if I still really wanted to do this. I replied that I was still interested, and they instructed me to set up a time for the recruiter to come back to the house so they could sign the documents.

They signed the official papers a few days later, and within three weeks, I was back on the bus from Oceanside to Los Angeles. I passed the physical exam and signed the contract for the job with the ASA and all the other required documents. With a group of about twenty others on May 29, 1976, I raised my right hand and said, "I do" as part of the oath of enlistment required to become a member of the United States Army. I had signed and sworn in for the delayed-entry program, which meant that I wouldn't leave for basic training and actually begin my three years of active duty until July 19, 1976. That was a little more than four weeks after my high school graduation day, and a little less than two months before my eighteenth birthday. My enlistment was for a total of six years. After my first three years of active duty, I would transition to three years inactive duty—susceptible to being called up to active or reserve duty at any time. I would be totally free from my commitment to the army on July 18, 1982.

CHAPTER THREE
Soldier, Manipulator (1976–1977)

Plunging into a totally foreign way of life

The entire time I went through the process of thinking about and then actually enlisting in the army, my relationship with Helen continued to deepen. And so did our conviction that seeing each other for only a few weeks at a time over the next three years wouldn't sidetrack our plan to be married at some point in the future. I honestly believed that the GI Bill benefits I would earn, the experience I'd gain from the job experience, and a top-secret level security clearance would all work together to make it possible for our future marriage to start on solid footing. What I didn't know at the time was how much I would miss having her present in my life on a daily basis and what that longing would eventually provoke me to do.

The day before the flight the army had arranged to take me to New Jersey for basic training, they took me, along with a number of other San Diego–area recruits, by bus, from Oceanside to the AFEES station in downtown Los Angeles. My parents and Helen decided to drive up to the hotel where I was to spend the night prior to the bus ride to LAX at five o'clock the next morning. By the time my bus arrived, they were already there, sitting in the lobby. As soon as I checked in and took my belongings to my room, I went back down to the lobby to say goodbye.

It was brutal. It was heart wrenching. It was far more difficult than I envisioned it would be. Seeing the depth of their sadness and knowing that *I* was the cause of this soul-piercing event crushed my own heart at a level I had never thought possible. After I shared tearful hugs with my parents and a big kiss with Helen, they headed out the door and down the street to where my dad had parked the car. I went up to the room that I would be sharing with another guy and looked out the window down at the street. Their car passed the front of the hotel, and I watched them until they went out of sight. For the first time in my life, I feared that I had made a mistake of life-changing proportions for me and the ones I loved.

When the four of us fresh-faced recruits from California landed in Philadelphia, we went straight to the location within the airport set aside for military personnel. There were about thirty other young men already there. They, too, had just arrived from other cities around the country and were also ready to begin their new lives as the property of Uncle Sam. We all waited for another hour or so while more men arrived and joined our ever-increasing group of recruits. We were then herded onto a couple of buses, and a few hours later, we drove through one of the gated entrances at Fort Dix, New Jersey.

As our bus came to a stop, we peered through the shaded windows and saw eight drill sergeants in their immaculately pressed olive-green fatigues and tightly shaved heads, on which those distinctive authority-declaring and new-recruit-intimidating, flat-brimmed hats rested. All of them had been in combat in Vietnam within the last few years, and the scowls on their faces sent shivers down my spine. The moment I stepped off the bus and my feet touched the ground, I came face to face with one of them. He yelled with a volume and intensity that made my former football coaches seem like cheerleaders. I swallowed hard, did what he told me to do, and almost buckled mentally and emotionally under the weight of realizing how unprepared I was for this radically different reality.

Intentional identity tampering

At one point, we were told to stand on the prepainted spaces on the asphalt and led in unison to a classroom inside a nearby building. With all of us sitting down at desks in neat rows, like in high school, uniformed leaders welcomed us. An officer stood before us and told us that although we were still American citizens, we had voluntarily joined an entity that had its own laws that we must abide by and, if necessary, be judged by. That class on the Uniform Code of Military Justice, also known as the UCMJ, was a wake-up call like no other.

Simply put, we were told that we not only had to abide by the laws of our country, but we would also be required to abide by the much more rigid standards that composed military law. They emphasized that the consequences of breaking the military's laws would be swift, powerful, and corrective. We were also told that we had surrendered our individual rights and would be required to go wherever our superiors told us to go and do whatever they told us to do, even if by doing so, we would forfeit our very lives. Everything else they explained about being government property was demonstrated by the experience of basic training.

I don't think any of us had an accurate understanding of what basic training would be like or what it was designed to accomplish prior to actually going through it. We were all typical young men of the mid-1970s. Most of us had fairly long hair worn it in whatever style we wanted, and our clothes were an expression of our individual personalities and preferences. As we were marched over to the barber shop and waited in long lines to sit down at one of the five or so barber's chairs, I knew I was saying goodbye to my wavy, beneath-the-collar-length hair. It was funny, the number of guys who actually replied with a style when the smirking barber asked them how much they would like taken off and what style they preferred. Their expressions were classic when the barbers would tell them they would give them personalized haircuts because it's the "new army." When they proceeded to run the electric trimmers from the center of their forehead to the back of their neck, leaving a trail about two inches wide, with not one hair left that was more than an eighth of an inch in length, the looks on some of their faces were priceless.

From those haircuts that each of us experienced, which made all of us appear similar, to being given the same underwear, socks, shoes, boots, uniforms, and hats, it was clear from the first few days of basic training that the army was intentionally crushing out the cultural values we had all been raised with. The idea that our individual identity and expression was the most important thing in life was methodically dismantled. It was an extremely uncomfortable process of remolding that took place every moment of every day, for seven straight weeks. That introductory season of preparation for a life that was so foreign to us generated disorientation, discouragement, frustration, and anger—at the very same time we were experiencing moments of excitement, exhilaration, and satisfaction at a level we'd never tasted before

Some of the guys resisted the process of having their individuality and identity modified and just didn't care when their expressions of individual rebellion resulted in severe consequences not only for them, but for their fellow members of their squad or platoon as well. Eventually, most of them finally did submit enough to continue on and graduate, but the few that just would not get with the program were forced out of the army and rewarded with a less-than-honorable or dishonorable discharge.

When the "lights out" order was given the night before graduation day, I got into my bunk and tried to sleep, but I couldn't keep my mind from processing all that I had been through since the day I arrived at Ft. Dix. I began analyzing both the training and myself from angles that I really never had before, and I noticed a few things.

At some point in the fourth or fifth week, a transition took place. The drill sergeants gradually stopped trying to break us down and threatening to boot us out. Instead, they began to encourage us that we were getting close to the finish line. They told us that becoming a real soldier, with all of the honor and benefits that come with that status, was only a few weeks away. They also began emphasizing the bigger purpose our training would serve in our own lives, our fellow soldiers' lives, our families, and, of course, our country. They focused on the importance of our graduation ceremony and how successful completion of the training would earn us the right and the honor to participate in that sacred event. They explained that the ceremony wasn't primarily for the family that might attend, or for themselves, as the leaders who trained us. They made clear that its primary purpose was for us, the graduates. It would serve as both a confirmation and a declaration to us, to our fellow soldiers, and to the world, that we had willfully and successfully made the transition from our primary identity as being individual to being a significant and necessary member of a group whose mission was perhaps more significant than any other organization in America.

As I pondered a little more deeply about this new facet of identity that would fully embrace me as the result of the graduation ceremony the next day, I knew that I would once again experience the joyful satisfaction produced by an unknown itch-for-identity being scratched.

The label "soldier" was about to be added to my existing identities as a member of the Jackson family and the boyfriend of Helen. I realized at that moment that the day-to-day emotional, mental, and physical demands of the previous seven weeks had dulled my ability to understand and enjoy the much deeper, broader, and more unique measure of satisfaction produced by the group identity that completing basic training ushered me into.

From the day I swore in until that final night before graduation, I had kept interpreting the army's advertising slogan, "Be all that you can be…in the army," as if it meant that becoming a member would reinforce or even amplify my individuality. But now I knew I had misunderstood. Being all that I wanted to be required voluntarily joining an organization that existed for a purpose larger than the individual interests of its members. I was now part of a group comprised of people who were all willing to practice self-denial and interdependence, within which each person willfully chose to permit the primary source of his identity to transition from himself to the group he was now an integral part of. In addition, even though I was still only seventeen years old when I graduated from basic training, it had become very obvious to me, and almost all of my fellow recruits, that it would be impossible to have an effective military built upon the cultural principles of the very people that we existed to protect.

Another identity label and conclusions drawn

The next morning as I was polishing my shoes and the brass insignia I would be wearing on my dress greens,

I couldn't keep my mind from going back to the principles of identity that I had contemplated the night before. I rewound to the day we got off the bus from the Philadelphia airport and began to see all that had taken place through the identity-sensitive lens I now possessed. As I did so, a specific moment during mail call that took place during the fourth or fifth week was triggered in my memory. By that point in the training, all of us had adjusted to the way the mail, and most official written correspondence from the army, was distributed to us.

Every morning, the entire company would gather in formation, organized by platoons, and would stand at attention. Announcements were made to the whole group by the company commander, and the drill sergeants that lead each platoon gave specific announcements to those they were directly leading. When that was finished, a stack of mail that sometimes included official mail from the army was handed to them. With every member of the platoon still standing at attention, the drill sergeants would pull off the top piece of mail and read the person's name it was addressed to. When your name was called, you'd loudly acknowledge your presence, take a coordinated step backward and then run behind all of the other guys who were side to side with you until you got to the end of the row. Then, you'd make your way up to the front and stand in front of the sergeant who had called out your name. At that point, he would usually make some sort of smart comment about the person named in the return-address section or criticize you for something you had done wrong during training the day before.

On that particular day, the drill sergeant was handing out official-looking manila-colored envelopes that contained information about the school and unit we were scheduled to join after we had completed basic training. As he looked at the next envelope in his hand, his eyebrows raised and his lips tightened, and then he called out, "Jackson." I had no idea what was going on, but I figured it must be really bad news for me. When I stood in front of him, he handed me the envelope, cocked his head a little to the left and scowled at me. He then told me he now knew that I was going to be in the ASA, and that he didn't like "spooks."

I couldn't get a totally clear read on what he was actually communicating, but it did make me feel like he was acknowledging that I was going to be part of a special entity that he didn't know much about. When I swore in, I realized I would be joining a unique unit after I went to basic, but until that moment, I didn't grasp that although most of the rest of the soldiers in the army were aware of ASA, they had no understanding of what it actually did. Because it was a very small part of the biggest branch of our military and since much of what those in ASA did was classified, the vast majority of drill sergeants never had the opportunity to train ASA-bound recruits. But clearly, when they did, it caught their attention, and they felt like they needed to make a comment about an outfit they probably knew less about than any other unit in the army. By time I was standing back in the midst of the formation, I was feeling really good and realized why: I'd just felt another identity-itch-scratching moment.

A quick trip home

When I got back to the barracks and opened that envelope, I saw that my orders required me to report to Fort Devens, Massachusetts. This was almost two weeks after the day we were scheduled to graduate, so I immediately decided to make a quick trip back home. It didn't matter that I would be squeezing in a back-and-forth cross-country flight of almost five thousand miles before checking in at a base that was less than three hundred miles from where I currently was. I was dying to see Helen and eager to reconnect with my mom and dad and the family back in Southern California. The ten days I spent there passed way too quickly, and my heart was heavy again as I boarded the flight for Boston. I tried to prepare myself, Helen, and the family for the reality that this time I could be away for close to one year. I didn't believe that I could take a break from the six months of training I was scheduled to receive at Ft. Devens, and I wasn't sure I'd have the opportunity to visit home prior to being sent to one of the bases overseas that the ASA operated on.

I had turned eighteen while I was home, and even though I was now officially both an adult and a member of the army, figuring out how to make the forty-five-mile trip from Logan Airport to Ft. Devens was anxiety producing. After picking up my duffel bag from the luggage carousel and stumbling around trying to find the right place to pick up the right bus, I finally had to ask for help from a few different people. It took me much longer than

I expected, but I eventually arrived at the main gate of Ft. Devens and reported in.

The weather was much cooler than what I had just left behind in San Diego, and the scenery we passed on the way was unlike anything we had in Southern California. Even though it was mid-September, some of the leaves had begun to change, and while my eyes swallowed up an aspect of nature's beauty I had never seen before, my heart was heavy with longing for Helen. My mind was in overdrive wondering if I actually had what it would take to complete the training successfully. Less than 50 percent of the people that began the schooling for the job skill that I was being trained for actually completed the course. What made the possibility of failure even more disheartening was the fact that if you couldn't make the grade, you would be transitioned to truck driver or cook training or—God forbid—infantry.

I was assigned to a specific company and placed into a four-person room in the barracks. It comprised people who were there for training in four different job specialties and were at different points in the process. I attended my first company formation at 6:00 a.m. on the first Monday I was there, and then those of us who were on day one of our training for our specialty were marched together as a group for a half mile or so down to where the school building stood. We were told that a few of the key components of the training were self-paced and that because there was such a need for our specialty at almost every field station overseas, a one-rank promotion would be given to the first person who was able to complete the course in less than six months. At the time, I was an E-1, the lowest rank in the army. By virtue of time in service, I was scheduled to make E-2 just a little more than halfway through the six months of schooling I had ahead of me. When I heard about this incentive, I decided I would be as diligent as I could be and would try to finish first and bag that promotion.

For me, the schooling required just the right amount of academic knowledge, new skill acquisition, and typing proficiency. My ability to type at forty-five words per minute prior to starting made it fairly easy for me to pass the sixty-word-per-minute requirement. I was also fairly good at memorizing, so I didn't have too much trouble with that facet of the training either. Within about eight weeks of beginning, I started to move ahead of schedule and found out that I was in front of everyone else.

A poem for an army buddy

About that time, one of my best buddies who knew and appreciated my sense of humor and love for writing asked me to write a poem to put on a plaque he planned to give to his dad for his birthday in February. He said that the previous spring and summer his dad had started preparing his boat for bass fishing season but had taken too long getting it ready and wasn't able to use it before the season closed. He wanted to give his dad a good-natured reminder of what a procrastinator he was and how it even impacted the thing he loved to do most—fishing. I came up with the following and gave it to my buddy on January 10, 1977:

You started before March; you were gonna be ready;
you worked very hard at a pace very steady.

But the weekends came, over and over,
and by the time you were done, it was now October.

The time went too fast; it really zipped;
you didn't make it out, but you were equipped.

So enjoy the winter, and drink lots of beer,
cause your stuff is all ready for the upcoming year.

He loved what I had come up with but said that it
would cost him an arm and a leg to put that much text
on a plaque, so he asked me if I could shorten it. This
is what I came up with that was placed on the plaque:

You worked all summer; your labor was great
But you took too long; now you'll have to wait

With the two-week Christmas break just around the
corner, I discovered that I could squeeze another short
trip home, so I flew back and forth across the country
once again. I only had five full days on the ground,
but that time with Helen and the family was worth the
money I spent and the jet lag I experienced. While I was
there, I discovered that my brother, Rick, and her sister
Marie (who had been dating the whole time Helen and
I were) were planning on being married near the end of
March. He wanted me to be his best man. I told them
that I wasn't sure if I would have enough leave time built

up, but if I did, I would definitely make the trip across the country to be there. When I left for the airport, even though it was now the third major farewell, it wasn't getting any easier, and I was discouraged the first few days I was back at the base.

A goal achieved, a promotion earned

Once we began classes again on the first Monday of January 1977, my mind was clicking on all cylinders. My recall of what I was reading, my ability to decipher and understand all we were being taught, my capacity to take what was coming in through my ears (by way of my headphones) and transcribe it onto paper through my fingers typing at a speed I never dreamed I could attain kept me in a constant state of amazement and gave me an ever-increasing amount of confidence.

The scheduled graduation date for my batch of students to complete the six-month course was mid-April. By the middle of January, I was convinced—and so were my teachers and trainers—that I could finish the entire course by the end of February, which would be six weeks ahead of schedule. And that's exactly what unfolded. I passed the final test on the last week of February. I was given a special graduation ceremony, received my orders to serve at Misawa Air Base, Japan, for eighteen months, and then entered the specialized preparation for the mission of the ASA Field Station there in northern Japan. Even though I had just gotten promoted to E-2 based on time in service nineteen days prior, I was still given the promised promotion to E-3 as a reward for finishing first in my class, weeks earlier than the scheduled finish date.

A manipulator at work

When I was home for Christmas a few months earlier, Helen and I had talked once again about the reality we knew would be a possibility from the beginning—that I could be sent overseas for a year and a half. When I received my orders to Misawa, I called her, and through our tears, we talked about how we felt now that it was going to become a reality. One of the things she mentioned in that conversation was her desire to stop taking the pill while I was gone so her body could return back to normal. I told her I thought that was a good idea, and then the conversation moved on. But over the next few days, I became increasingly distressed and discouraged by the thought of being away from her on the other side of the world for that long.

I was still convinced that our being married at a future point in time was going to take place. But now, that conviction fueled, unleashed, and amplified a natural ability I had learned that I possessed during the previous few years. Through a number of circumstances, I had become consciously aware of my capacity to exert influence over other people. Or to put it another way, I figured out I had a talent for manipulation and was well on my way to becoming a master at it.

It seemed like no matter what the impulse was, if I really wanted something that I believed would make me happy, my mind automatically began concocting a scheme to obtain it. And in most cases, this scheme required convincing other people of certain things to move them to make the decisions I wanted them to make in order to produce the outcome I desired, which always benefited me.

Troubled to the core by the realistic possibility that I could be separated for a year and a half from the beautiful young woman that I knew would be my wife, the scheme factory in my mind began working at maximum capacity as soon as I hung up the phone. Within hours, I had a blueprint that included a simple plan A, and just in case that didn't work, a much more manipulative and complex plan B. Both plans hinged on my ability to convince someone else to do something that was the polar opposite of common sense and, if chosen by her, would probably subject her to severe criticism from other people.

I didn't move forward with the plan immediately because I understood that if successful, it would produce life-changing implications for more than just Helen and me. Despite the fact that what I was learning in school about the job I was set to do in Japan required serious concentration, I couldn't stop analyzing both plans, trying to figure out every possible outcome for both of them, and then refining what my response should be for each scenario. Five days after the first call that was generated by my orders to Misawa, I nervously sat down at the pay phone in the barracks and began dialing Helen's number.

After getting caught up on everyone's reaction to the news about me being sent to Japan and clarifying that there was no one within earshot of her, I told her about all the things that had consumed my thinking since the last time we talked. And then I revealed plan A to her: I would ask her mom for permission for us to be married that summer. I would return for a short visit for the wedding, and then the two of us would leave for Japan a few days later.

She said that there was no way her mom—or any other mom for that matter—would ever give approval for their sixteen-year-old daughter, in her sophomore year of high school, to marry an eighteen-year-old soldier boy, much less one who would then take her to the other side of the world a few days after their wedding. Of course, I knew that was exactly how Helen would view the possibility of plan A succeeding. After she had finished explaining this, I told her I was still going to give it a try, knowing there was a 99 percent guarantee of failure.

She then asked me what my plan B was. I hesitated for a few seconds and asked her to wait until I had finished unpacking the details before she responded. She agreed. I told her that since she already wanted to go off the pill during my absence, she could stop taking it immediately—that day if possible. And then, when we came together while I was back home for a few days prior to leaving for Japan, and if her body had adjusted back to normal by then, she just might wind up being pregnant. If that happened, we would have the greatest leverage possible to try to convince her mom to give us permission to be married and get on board with my plan to begin our married life together in Japan.

She shared her concerns. I told her I understood them, but I also gave her a variety of reasons for not letting her concerns move her away from doing the things now that could help the future we dreamed about become a reality much sooner than we had ever considered. The call ended with her saying that she needed a few days to think about it. A couple of days later, we talked again, and she said she was willing to go for it. When I hung up the phone, I felt extremely happy, but also mildly disturbed by the way I had pressured Helen to get on board with a plan that required her to carry the bulk of the load in order for it to succeed.

I called her mom a week or so later and proposed plan A to her. As any mother in her right mind would, she said there was no way she could agree to what I was asking and was offended that I would even ask her something like that. I attempted one more time to get her to change her mind and failed miserably, and I knew that I had probably increased her distaste for me. I had expected that conversation to go the way that it did, so I wasn't distressed at the conclusion of the call. In fact, it was exhilarating to know that her denial was the gate opener that made it possible for Helen to walk with me together down the other path that I had created, hoping to reach the destination that the two of us longed for.

A wedding planned

With plan B now firmly in place and proceeding, the weeks that I spent finishing up my specialized training at Ft. Devens were both exciting and inspiring. About three weeks before I headed for Logan Airport for the last time, I learned that my two best buddies would finish the course in the allotted time, and that both of them would be stationed at Okinawa. As it turned out, I was the only one from our batch of students that was given orders to go to Misawa. If the plan with Helen wasn't already in motion and the desired outcome not a real possibility, I probably would have been discouraged by learning that I would spend at least the next year and a half at a base very far from where my two best buddies were. And even though the plan was just as likely to fail as it was to succeed, the fact that it had a reasonable possibility of succeeding eased the level of sadness I felt as I said goodbye to them.

Finishing the course early and being granted extra leave time due to my upcoming eighteen-month tour in Japan made it possible for me to arrive back in Escondido a few days before Rick and Marie's wedding. Helen enjoyed being Marie's maid of honor, and I loved being Rick's best man, but the plot that I had concocted consumed most of my thinking. Helen had followed through with her contribution to the plan, and our time together was sweeter than it had ever been. But as pleasurable and meaningful as my visit was, the reality that a pregnancy wasn't guaranteed cast a shadow on my time there that only the two of us could see. We had both agreed to not tell anyone about what we were doing, which was much easier for me to follow through with than her.

At the end of my leave, Helen and my mom and dad once again drove me to the place I needed to be in order to proceed with my career in the army. In this case, we went all the way from Escondido to Travis Air Force Base, near San Francisco. It was another heavy and tearful goodbye for all of us, especially my parents because they believed that they wouldn't see me again for eighteen months. But because of what Helen and I knew might be discovered within the next two months, the fog of sadness that the moment should have produced wasn't as dense as it could have been.

My mind was exploding with dozens of overlapping thoughts as I buckled my seat belt and felt the thrust of that Flying Tiger aircraft taking off and hurdling through the air much further westward than I had ever been. Almost three days later, I was escorted to my room in the army barracks section of Misawa Air Base and introduced to my roommate. After being given the orientation to the Army Security Agency Field Station Misawa command structure, I was then transported up to the operations center that was referred to as "the hill." I shadowed someone else for a few days and within a week of my arrival began working at one of the positions as an operator.

I wanted to call Helen every week, but the three-dollar-per-minute charge pretty much killed that desire, so we talked every two weeks for no more than fifteen minutes. A little more than two months after I arrived, she was able to obtain a pregnancy test—and it was positive! When she told me, it was the greatest news I had ever heard up to that moment in my life. But my joy was almost immediately dampened by the fact that I wouldn't be there with her when she told her mom that she was going to have a baby. And even more so by the reality that she could refuse to give her legal consent for her underage daughter to be married and there would be nothing we could do about it.

After a few days of thinking through how she was going to tell her mom, she finally did. She also pleaded with her to permit us to be married as soon as possible and then go with me back to Japan a few days after the wedding. As we both expected, her mom was caught totally by surprise and said that she needed some time to think about it herself and then discuss it with Helen's dad before making her decision. A little more than a week later, her mom still hadn't decided, so I took the initiative to call her and try to convince her, bringing to bear all the leverage that I could muster.

I told her that it wasn't a loser that was asking for permission to marry her daughter. I was a high school graduate that had been accepted to go to a university, but chose to serve my country instead. I reminded her that I had qualified to become a part of an elite unit that required me to be granted a top-secret clearance and had passed a thorough background investigation of my character and behavior by the Department of Defense to obtain that level of clearance.

I described how I had also finished first in my job training school and gotten a promotion as a result. I said that If I chose to be discharged after the end of my enlistment, there was a very strong possibility that I would be offered a very good job within the federal government. And finally, trying to sound as manly and confidently as I could, I stated that with my salary and benefits, I would be able to provide all of the things necessary for her daughter to have the comfortable life that she wanted and deserved. After listening silently to all of the reasons why I thought she should go along with our plan, her mom concluded her side of the conversation by telling me that she was going to continue to think about it.

Helen called me a few days later and told me that despite having some serious reservations, her mom and dad had both agreed to the scenario we had mapped out. She also said they had already started planning our wedding which needed to take place less than seven weeks later because she wouldn't be given permission to fly if she was more than five months along in the pregnancy.

Because I had only accrued ten days of leave and wanted to make a trip back to the States less than four months after my arrival in Misawa, I needed special permission from my commanding officer. Even though I was reluctant to do it, I knew that I had to tell him the real reason for the trip in order for my unorthodox request to be granted. He hesitated at first, cleared his throat, and asked me a couple of thought-provoking questions. He finally agreed to let me go but warned me that he'd seen many young soldiers do what I was about to do, and very few of their marriages turned out the way they thought they would.

CHAPTER FOUR

Husband, Father, Civilian (1977–1980)

Adding another layer of identity

With my leave granted, our wedding day was scheduled for Friday, July 22, 1977. Because I had been hoping from the day I had left that things would unfold just like this, I researched our housing options and discovered that it wasn't possible for us to live on base. With that reality in mind, a few weeks before I left, I found a nice two-bedroom house to rent in the part of Misawa that was just outside one of the lesser-used gates that led on to the base.

I didn't tell my company commander, and neither Helen nor I told anyone else that her pregnancy was actually part of a master plan, birthed out of our complete confidence that we would spend the rest of our lives together as husband and wife. It seemed to both of us that being viewed as young people stepping up to the plate and demonstrating an incredible step of maturity in response to a surprise event was preferable to being viewed as young people who were so arrogant and prideful that they thought they could do something that no one in their right mind would ever give their approval to.

In the midst of having to adjust to being pregnant and all that goes along with it, and with the help of her mom and other family members, she applied for and received a passport in her maiden name and took care of all of the marriage license details. By the time I arrived back in Escondido six days before the wedding, everything was planned and ready. I felt incredibly guilty about not being able to help with any of it, but there was nothing I could do from eight thousand miles away.

The first time I saw her after arriving, it was clear that her natural beauty was amplified even more by being pregnant. And the moment I laid eyes on her in that beautiful white wedding dress at the arm of her dad as they entered the church and began walking down the aisle toward me, a wave of joy and satisfaction like none I'd ever experienced overcame me. Seeing her nervous smile behind the veil, and the way that small but noticeable belly bump pushed the dress outward in her midsection, provoked a depth of love for her that was literally indescribable. As the ceremony proceeded, I couldn't take my eyes off her.

After saying "I do" to the declaration of commitment and then hearing her do the same, I was consciously aware and totally overwhelmed by the fact that the moment I had dreamed about since the first time I saw her was now a reality. After I lifted her veil and kissed her, we were prayed for and then introduced to those in attendance as Mr. and Mrs. Jeffrey Jackson. Hearing that and then a few minutes later having everyone refer to us as Jeff and Helen as they congratulated us, it dawned on me that this was the latest and by far the greatest of the identity-itch-scratching moments that I had experienced.

On Sunday, two days after our wedding, our parents escorted us to LAX for our flight to Japan. I had already done this a few times, and the knowledge that she was going with me made the goodbye easier than it had ever been for me. But it was absolutely crushing for her. A number of firsts had come upon both of us over the previous few months, but she had experienced many more than I had. She was pregnant, married, flying, leaving behind her family and country, and committing herself fully into my care—all for the very first time. While she wept gently and silently in the seat next to me as the thrust of the 747 launched us skyward, I knew that the depth of her trust in me and the weight of the responsibility I now had as a husband, and soon-to-be father, would require a level of self-denial that I wasn't sure I possessed, but which I longed for with every fiber of my being.

Marriage, pregnancy, fatherhood

It wasn't easy to learn how to live together as a married couple at the same time we were learning how to live in a house and in a community that was radically different than anything either of us had ever experienced. Those challenges actually required a level of combined effort that connected us with each other at a depth that I think every married couple envisions they'll attain after their wedding day. Because everything we encountered and needed to master was new to both of us, we shared the frustration of not understanding how to do certain things and the feeling of satisfaction when we figured out how to do something that neither of us had ever done before. The context within which we began our married life would have driven a dagger of death into the heart of our relationship if we had resisted the level of inter-dependence the situation demanded.

A huge part of the context that we were forced to adjust to was my army-ordered work schedule. In every twenty-four-day block of time we were there, I worked six straight day shifts, six straight afternoon-evening shifts, and then six straight graveyard shifts with two days off between each set of six. This meant that Helen was alone at home outside the boundaries of the base until 11:30 p.m. for six straight nights, and then from 10:45 p.m. to 7:30 a.m. for another six straight nights every month. When that fact of life is coupled with the reality that the temperature was always cold enough to produce the fourteen feet of snow we received that winter, the strength she displayed to not only survive but thrive despite those obstacles reinforced the amazement I always felt that a young woman of her character and caliber would actually love and commit herself to a guy as goofy as I was.

One of the things that kept me from being crippled with worry about her while she was alone at home was the culture of the Japanese people in general and spe-cifically in and around the city of Misawa. Even before I made the flight back home to marry her and bring her back with me, I had spent a lot of time in the city and had even done some sightseeing dozens of miles away from the base. I knew that the crime rate, especially violent crime, was almost nonexistent. The time that I spent walking around with my buddies, eating in restaurants, checking out the stores, and even taking the train to other parts of northern Japan to sightsee or witness cultural events all meshed together to convince me that leaving Helen alone all night in our house in a small Japanese city was less of a risk than it would be in just about any city outside a military base in my own country.

Once we were comfortably settled in our house and the routine of my crazy work schedule became familiar, Helen and I and another buddy, who also had a young wife who was pregnant, began spending most of our nonwork time immersed in exploring life outside the base. I was intrigued by the culture of Japanese people and how similar some of its foundational values and traits were to the culture of the US military. I came to believe that if an American serviceman didn't just tolerate military life, but embraced it and found fulfillment in it, a cultural severing or disconnection from his own countrymen who weren't in the military was inevitable. And as hard as it was to believe, a military person like that would have values and behaviors more in common with the people of Japan and their culture than he did with the very people he was sworn to protect.

From the day we arrived together in Misawa until the night she went into labor a few days after Christmas, I loved and cherished our life together as a married couple. I was thoroughly excited about the birth of our child even though I recognized the time we had to live together as just the two of us was about to come to an end for at least another eighteen years. And like normal, my naturally calculating mind had already determined that even though we would probably have more children later on, if we did stop after the birth of this one, we would still be very young when our child reached adulthood. I would be only thirty-seven, and she'd be only thirty-five years old, if the bundle of joy that was about to enter our lives went off to college or into the military after graduating high school at the age of eighteen.

Because Misawa was a comparatively small base with less than four thousand troops stationed there, the hospital reflected that and offered very basic medical care. An average of three babies per month were delivered there, which made it very easy to get to know the OB/GYN and nursing staff on a personal level as the pregnancy moved along. Helen was in hard labor for just under three hours, and on the evening of December 29, 1977, we had the joy of welcoming a beautiful baby boy, Travis Paul Jackson, into our lives. Once he was out of the womb, they did the routine medical checks done to a newborn baby, including a blood test. He was slightly yellowish due to a bit of jaundice, which was fairly normal, but because of that, when Helen wasn't feeding him, he needed to be kept in an incubator under lights.

A short-lived moment of joy, a crisis-generated journey

The next day, the doctor informed us that the results of the blood tests they ran on the baby showed a problem that could be serious. His platelet count was much less than it should have been, and it continued to decrease each time they did a blood test on him. They couldn't release him until things changed, and they kept a very close watch on him over the next two days. Each day, the doctor would report that his platelet count was continuing to diminish. On the afternoon of the fourth day, he told us to go home and pack some clothes because he was going to put our son on an air force air ambulance flight to Yokota Air Force Base near Tokyo the very next morning. He assured us that the specialists and resources at the large hospital there would be better able to determine what specifically was happening. Hearing that, our worry level climbed even higher.

The doctor had contacted my company commander, informed him of what was happening, and asked him to permit me to go with my wife and son. He graciously signed the order that was needed, and the next morning we boarded a C-141 air force cargo plane that had been built out to be a flying medical ward. The wooden seats with small cushions for healthy passengers faced the back of the plane; this made it possible to see the medical staff taking care of the patients being transported. Gurney-type beds had been attached to the sides of the fuselage on both sides. Our son was still being kept in an incubator. They brought him in on a wheeled cart and strapped it down onto one of the beds.

When we landed at Yokota AFB, we rode in the ambulance that transported our son in the incubator to the base hospital. They examined him, checked his blood again, and about an hour later, informed us that his condition was beyond their capacity to help him. They told us they were sending us to Tripler Army Hospital in Honolulu, Hawaii, which had the best neonatal unit in the entire Pacific region. Within minutes, we were in the ambulance once again and taken back to the same flying medical transport aircraft we had just deplaned from. It was still sitting on the tarmac, being loaded up with fuel, supplies, and patients that were being transferred to other air force bases. Our son was the final patient put on board, and once we saw his incubator had been locked securely into place, and the rear door had been raised and secured, we put wax ear plugs in once again, and away we went.

Once we were airborne, and the medical staff was able to move around and care for the patients, one of them came over to us and explained what was happening. She said that we were on board an air force medical evacuation vessel that served the Far East. Our final destination would eventually be Hickam Air Force Base in Honolulu, at which time our son would be ground transported to Tripler Army Hospital, per the orders of the doctors at Yokota. We wouldn't arrive at our destination until we had stopped at a number of air force bases scattered across the Pacific region. Even having heard her explain the itinerary, we had no idea how long the journey to Hawaii would actually take.

An hour or so after we left Yokota, we landed at Kadena AFB in Okinawa. A few people were placed on board there, and then we took off again. Hours later, we landed and took off from three different bases in Korea—Osan, Pusan, and Seoul. At close to 10:00 p.m.

that evening, we landed at Clark AFB in the Philippines. Once the engines of the plane had shut down, we were told that this was the overnight stop on the journey, with the flight continuing on to the next stop at 6:00 a.m. They informed us that all patients would be transferred to the base hospital, and accommodations would be made for accompanying family members.

A crescendo reached, a journey continued

Once again, we rode in the ambulance with our son to the hospital and waited while the staff got him set up and ran blood tests. The doctor came out and told us that due to the seriousness of our son's condition, they preferred that we stay in the hospital with him, and not at the billeting facility where they normally housed people on a different part of the base. He told us to sit tight and that someone from the hospital would take us to a place where we could get some sleep. As we waited, our heads were spinning and our hopefulness felt like it was in a vice that was tightening ever so slowly and being squeezed to the point where it could burst at any moment.

A few minutes later, a supervisor came into the room and told us that their original plan was to let us sleep in an empty, two-patient room, but that it had been an extremely busy day and that wasn't possible. Because of that, the only two-patient room available in the whole hospital was on the psychiatric ward, and if we weren't agreeable to that, we would have to sleep as best as we could in the waiting room we were standing in at the moment. We were so wiped out that we quickly agreed to take the room they were offering on the psych floor.

I probably don't need to describe the look, behavior, and sounds being produced by the patients we encountered in the hallway as we were escorted to the room. After the supervisor left, we closed the door, and I hugged Helen as tight as I could and tried to comfort her at a level that I had never needed to before. We collapsed onto the beds, talked for a few minutes, and then drifted off to sleep.

A few hours later, around two o'clock in the morning, there was a firm knock on the door, and I groggily made my way over and opened it. The orderly told me that the doctors needed to speak with us as soon as possible and that we needed to get dressed quickly and follow him back to the neonatal nursery. We did what we were told, and gripping one another's hands as firmly as possible, we walked into the nursery waiting room.

A doctor whom we hadn't recognized came in and told us to follow him into the area where our son was sleeping in the incubator. Once we were standing next to the incubator, the doctor told us that his platelets had continued to decrease and had just passed a point that made his blood so thin that it could just seep through the walls of his veins and arteries. He said if it happened in his brain, it could be fatal. He solemnly advised us that if we were religious people, we should seek out a spiritual leader for help to prepare us for the possible worst-case scenario.

The doctor's words were the final, hurricane-force wind gust to push us over the emotional edge we had been teetering on since the pediatrician in Misawa sent us to Yokota thirty-six hours earlier. I held Helen even tighter than I had just a few hours before, as tears tumbled from my cheeks into her hair, and her tears soaked my neck and dampened my shirt. I hadn't yet learned to pray out loud, so I cried out to God silently, pleading with Him to keep our son alive.

A few minutes later I asked the staff for the number of the Catholic chaplain on base. I was amazed that although it was three o'clock in the morning, he answered before the third ring. It was obvious the call woke him up, but he was instantly attentive. I gave him a short summary of what was going on, and with an incredibly compassionate tone, he said that he would be at the hospital in about twenty minutes.

He arrived sooner than he had predicted. He looked younger than I expected and very distinguished in the dark-black priestly shirt and white collar. He walked right over to us and embraced us both at the same time. He held us firmly and silently for a few long minutes and then began praying for us and for Travis, loud enough for us to hear his words. Although neither of us had ever been in a situation like this before, it was clear that this chaplain had fine-tuned his ability to be a source of comfort and encouragement to people in the midst of crisis, and we were both thankful for his presence.

When he finished praying, he walked over to the nurse's station where the doctor was seated in the middle of a few nurses. We stayed close to the incubator so we couldn't hear their conversation. He walked back over to us and said that based on what the doctor told him, and his own faith that God was going to spare our son's life, he was only going to baptize Travis, and not perform any kind of last-rite ceremony. Hearing his confidence fanned the ember of hope that had almost burned out within both of us.

The chaplain asked the nurse if it would be possible, and safe, to slip a small plastic bottle of holy water into the incubator through the side opening. She said yes, and as she walked toward it, he pulled it out of his pants pocket and handed it to her. She opened the side flap, placed the bottle on the sheet next to Travis's head, and then closed and latched the flap. The priest then put his hands in through the round holes and into the rubber gloves that were attached to the inside of the round holes. He picked up the little bottle of holy water with his rubber-gloved hands and popped off the cap. He slipped his left hand gently under Travis's neck and lifted just enough so that the top of Travis's head was tilted back. Using his right hand, he reached over and squeezed out a small stream of holy water onto the top of the baby's head. As it flowed down onto the sheet, he prayed once again.

He softly removed his hands from under Travis's head and neck and pulled his hands out of the incubator. After the nurse handed the holy water bottle back to him, he told us that he didn't have any official baptismal certificates in his briefcase and began looking around the room. He spotted a paper towel dispenser mounted on the wall next to a sink and walked over to it. He pulled out one of those rough-to-the-touch, brown paper towels that was folded in the middle, and strolled back over to where we were standing next to the incubator. He laid it on the cover, pulled out his pen, and asked us for Travis's full name and place and date of birth. In beautiful penmanship, he wrote the date, January 6, 1978, on the top left corner, followed by Travis's biographical details and a declaration that he had baptized him. He signed the bottom right-hand side and added the words "Clark Air Base, Philippines" under his signature.

After he left, the hospital staff ran another blood test, and his platelet count had not decreased, so the nurses urged us to go out to the waiting area and try to get some sleep before the next leg of our journey to Hawaii, which had been moved back to 7:00 a.m. Neither one of us slept. We just sat next to each other and alternated between crying, holding hands, and talking about a variety of things so we wouldn't fixate on what might happen next with our firstborn.

He made it through the rest of the night, and we were all loaded back onto the plane, and away we went. Approximately four hours after takeoff, we landed at Andersen AFB in Guam—the last pickup point on the path to Hawaii. As great as it was to hear the news that our next stop was the final one, our happiness and relief were dampened when they said it would take a little more than nine more hours to get there. By the time we touched down at Hickam AFB on Oahu, it had been forty-one hours since we left Yokota AFB, almost twenty-four of those spent in the air.

When we were at Yokota and had been told that we were being sent to Hawaii, we called our families and told them what was happening and where we were headed. As long and arduous as the trip around the Pacific was for us, it gave both of our families enough time to book flights and arrive in Honolulu almost a full twenty-four hours before we did. Our parents, my brother, her two sisters, and even her grandmother had already checked in at a hotel, rented a car, and were able to meet us at Tripler Army Hospital. They arrived a few moments after the ambulance ride with Travis from Hickam.

The army found a room for Helen and me in the officers' billeting across the street from the hospital, and all of our family members waited for us in the hospital as we checked in to our room and took showers. By the time we went back to the special nursery area where Travis was being treated, they had already done blood tests, and the specialists had examined him thoroughly. They moved him from the incubator to a crib-type bed that was akin to a small hospital bed, sitting higher above the ground than normal. They finally let us hold him in our arms for the first time since his birth. We were both overwhelmed with a joy that words can't possibly describe.

We held him for a while, and after the nurse told us to go ahead and lay him down so they could run some more tests on him, a doctor walked in and invited us to follow him. He led us to his office, where a second doctor was standing, reviewing a file that had our son's name on it. They sat us down and summarized the situation with Travis as they had come to understand it.

Our son spared, a father once again

They began by telling us how sorry they were that the route to Tripler had taken so long and how heartbreaking it must have been for us. They then said they were happy to report that his platelet count on arrival was the same as it was when we left Clark AFB. At that point, they told us that the problem had one of two possible causes. First, it could have been that his bone marrow had only produced the original number of platelets he was born with and then stopped producing any more. If that was the case, it was a fairly rare disorder that would require a complete blood transfusion approximately once a year for the rest of his life. Or second, it could have been that his marrow was producing the platelets, but for some unknown reason, they weren't being released and disbursed throughout his system.

They told us they hoped it was the latter, and they were planning on performing different testing, starting immediately. The main things they wanted us to know at that moment in time were that his life was no longer in danger, and his life span would be as normal as everyone else's. They also told Helen that if she wanted to begin breastfeeding him again, she could start doing so as soon as she'd like to—which is exactly what she did shortly after that conversation, and then every three to four hours from then onward.

The next afternoon, when we entered the nursery after having lunch with the family, the doctor approached us just as Helen sat down to feed Travis. His demeanor was much lighter than it was the day before. He said that they had given a few doses of fresh frozen plasma to Travis, as the first attempt at discovering the source of the problem. He then told us that after the third dose, his platelet count skyrocketed to the level that it should be, and with no further doses given, his count had remained constant.

He said that the best way to describe it was that his marrow was like a locked treasure chest that actually was producing platelets and that, apparently, the fresh frozen plasma was like a key that had been inserted that unlocked and opened it. He said his plan was to keep testing Travis's blood every few hours for the rest of the day and night, and if it stayed at the level he expected, he would release him, contingent upon us bringing him back to the hospital every eight hours for blood tests. He also said that he wanted to follow that plan for at least four days, and if his platelet count stayed at the right level, he'd sign the papers for Travis to be released, and we would be sent back to Misawa to continue our life and duty there.

Travis's levels wound up looking good the next day, so they released him to us. We spent every moment of the next few days with our little bundle of joy and the family that had made the trip to see us, making sure to get him back to the hospital on time for his blood test and checkups. On the day our family members had previously scheduled to head back to the mainland, the doctor signed the final release for us to return to Japan. The army booked us to fly back to Tokyo and then on to Misawa on commercial flights, the day after we were to say goodbye to all of them at the Honolulu International Airport.

Back in Misawa, we had his blood checked every week for a month, and since everything remained normal, they told us to raise him like any other healthy baby boy, and that's what we did. That first time we entered our house with our son, I experienced another identity-itch-scratching moment. Adding the role of father to my fairly new identity as a husband, and the responsibility that came with being both, was sobering, but deeply fulfilling. This latest facet of my identity felt just right, and I knew that I would embrace it fully and cherish it passionately for the rest of my life.

We adjusted to life back in Misawa as a family of three and developed a rhythm within a few weeks of our return. Seven months later, I received orders for my next duty station at Kelly Air Force Base in San Antonio, Texas. As much as I was loving every moment of life with my little family, when we talked about the different options we had for the transition, a penny-pincher trait of mine kicked in. To save money and to give the family back home some extra time with Helen and Travis before we made the drive to Texas, we made the decision for her and Travis to return a full month before my departure date. They left a week before my twentieth birthday in mid-September—just a few days after we discovered that Helen was pregnant with our second child. A few hours after the flight from Misawa to Tokyo departed, I moved into a two-man room in the barracks and tried to squeeze my belongings into the few existing places that the other occupant hadn't already monopolized. Before I finally fell asleep that night, I realized that my tightwad tendencies had moved me to do something that I was already beginning to regret. I was miserable for every one of those thirty-two days, and even up until this point of my life, my twentieth birthday was the worst I've ever had. I felt totally incomplete, with no real joy, and my birthday phone call with Helen amplified my frustration with myself and increased my sadness. It took everything within me to not weep uncontrollably while talking with her, especially when she held the phone up so Travis could hear my voice, and he cooed in response.

About a month later, I reunited with Helen and our son and had the opportunity to spend seven days with the whole family. We piled our little family into the small Fiat station wagon given to us by Helen's dad and made the drive from Southern California to San Antonio in mid-October of 1978. Our first daughter, Jody Lynn, was born in March of 1979, and I received my honorable discharge from active duty a few months later on July 18. When we pulled into my parents' apartment complex after the two-day drive back to Escondido, I was twenty years old, with a beautiful eighteen-year-old wife, two healthy children, and three years of military service under my belt, eighteen months of which were spent in northern Japan.

A veteran in a civilian world

Helen and I had some level of awareness about the uniqueness of our situation as we began living life as a young family outside the familiar confines of the military. We were as prepared as possible for the amazement our old friends showed when we reconnected, and they discovered the difference between where they were in their lives and where we were in ours. After their initial expressions of surprise, it felt like most of them nonverbally expressed a skepticism about the possibility of our marriage being able to stand the test of time. A few of them were even bold enough to tell us what they were thinking, following their comments by telling us that they hoped we would beat the odds that were so clearly stacked against us. We recognized that was a logical thing for people to conclude based on the statistics, but we also knew that what we had was probably different than the others, and our dreams of growing old together would become a reality.

What we weren't prepared for as we plunged back into the vast ocean of American life was the awareness of how much we had been shaped and molded by military life and culture, and how difficult it would be to make the adjustment back into living among people who navigated with cultural values that were the almost complete opposite of those we'd adopted. As much as they tried to equip us, the few classes the army gave us to prepare us for life back in the civilian world were woefully inadequate.

Within weeks of our return, we came face to face with the reality that we had transitioned from a culture in which self-denial and self-sacrifice for the good of others is the highest virtue, back into a one that was bestowing an ever-increasing amount of honor upon pursuing self-fulfillment, self-love, and self-expression as the source of happiness and satisfaction. Although my identity as an active-duty soldier was now in the past, it was very clear to me that it was going to be impossible to wear the civilian title in the same way I had in the past, or to fully embrace the cultural values most Americans lived by. If it wasn't for the depth of connection I had with our family still living in the area, I could have been swallowed up by the negative effects that so many members of the military experience as a result of stepping back into the civilian world.

Less than a month after we arrived back in town, we rented a small two-bedroom duplex. Helen began working soon after, and a few days before my twenty-first birthday in September, I started attending classes at a business college. I used my GI Bill benefits to pursue a career as a state-certified court reporter. When I was five months into the two-year course, the school informed us that they had been purchased by a different business school.

For most people this was actually good news, but it was the worst possible news for me and the other students using GI Bill benefits. We were told that the school that purchased our school did not have proper VA certification, and it would take two years for them to obtain it. This meant that in order to continue, I would need to pay out of my own pocket, which was simply not possible. My only other option was to quit pursuing that career path and to find a full-time job. I knew that I would never be able to commit to being a full-time student without the need to also work, and I was okay with that.

CHAPTER FIVE

Born-Again Christian, Manager, Pastor (1980–1986)

Surrender and submission to Jesus

I found work almost immediately after attending my last class as a court-reporting student. I'd never had a problem landing a job; the problem I did have was that after I figured out how to do whatever job I had, and do it well, I got bored and began looking for a different job. If I found another one, and it paid a little more, I would quit and move on to that one.

I began taking night classes at a local community college in September of 1980. I was already on my third job since I was forced to quit the court-reporting school. My tuition and books were being paid for by my GI Bill benefits, and even though there were a few dollars left each month, I still needed to work full time to make ends meet. It was quite a balancing act for a few years with both of us working, making sure the kids were being cared for, and my cramming in at least two classes per semester, but we found a routine that made things work as smoothly as possible.

During this season of our lives, we continued to attend mass at our local Catholic church as often as possible. But as much as I wanted God to be real in my life, I knew in my heart of hearts that He really wasn't, and I was losing hope that following the same traditions I had grown up with would actually move me any closer to Him, or vice versa. While I was away in the army, my brother had a born-again Christian experience that completely altered the way he lived his life. When we were back in town, he explained to me what had happened a number of times, but I was convinced that while he needed something that radical to happen to him, I didn't.

To pacify him, Helen and I attended a Sunday-morning service at the church he and Helen's sister had been attending. It was a radically different way of doing church and didn't appeal to me in any way, shape, or form. They could tell we didn't like it and eventually backed off trying to slip Jesus into most of our conversations and inviting us to their church. But that one time we did attend, we had filled out a visitor card, and a few weeks later on a Monday night, there was a knock on our door. The two men standing there introduced themselves, told us how happy they were that we had visited their church, and asked if they could come in and talk with us. At that time in my life, I was hooked on Monday Night Football and really didn't like being interrupted when the game was on, but I let them in and called for Helen to join us in our living room.

JEFF JACKSON

Although I knew they might think it was rude, I didn't really care, so I turned the volume down on the TV but left the game on so I could keep an eye on what was happening while we talked. They explained the basics of the Gospel to us in a very thorough way, and I understood what they were saying even though I was keeping track of the game. But Helen gave them her full attention. After a forty-five-minute presentation, they asked if we wanted to accept Jesus as our Savior. We both said yes, and they led us in a prayer that we repeated verbatim. When we were finished, they told us that heaven would be guaranteed to us and that we would be experiencing life in a new way.

I was glad when we closed the door behind them on their way out so I could get back to the game. Although I wanted to take what had just occurred very seriously, I knew that the only reason I agreed with them was to get back to the game. I really didn't feel any different and had no desire to make any kind of changes in my life. What I didn't know until a few days later was that Helen had experienced something very real that night, and she sincerely meant what she had said in the prayer. Although she tended to follow my lead in church-related decisions, God was now at work in her life. She began reading the Bible and became even more selfless and loving than she had already been.

We continued in our life routines over the next year, including going faithfully to the Catholic church I had grown up attending, but something interesting began happening to me not too long after the night we both prayed with the two men from my brother's church. A

68

man I worked with told me that he had recently asked Jesus into his heart and had become a born-again Christian. Two months later, when I started the two new classes I was taking at the local community college, there were three or four people in each of my classes that were very vocal about their following of Jesus, and they were always trying to bring Jesus and the Gospels into every class discussion or conversation they had with any of the rest of us who were taking the class.

My initial reaction to what felt like a constant bombardment of people telling me these things was annoyance. They implied that they gave no credibility to the fact that I was a churchgoing Christian of the Catholic tradition. But when it kept happening in so many different ways, at so many different times, and through so many different people, I finally began to entertain the idea that God might actually be pursuing me, rather than waiting for me to seriously begin chasing after Him. It became clear that even though my brother and Helen's sister had backed off pestering me with the whole born-again thing, God was the one orchestrating these random people's efforts to share the same basic truths with me. I finally concluded that if that was the case, I needed to begin taking some initiative to study and discover what this experience they were describing was all about.

I knew that I didn't like the way my brother's church did their Sunday-morning service, so I began asking a few of my friends for another church to look into in order to understand what born-again people actually believe, why they believe it, and how they practice their faith. It really didn't surprise me when they recommended I check out the largest and most well-known evangelical church in our city.

A few weeks later, we attended one of their services after having attended mass earlier that morning. The bulletin they handed out referenced a four-week new-believer's class that would be starting the following Sunday morning, taking place during one of the regular worship services. That sounded like it would be a good place to begin to understand what they believed, so I decided to attend.

There were about twenty people in the class that was led by two men. They began by explaining what a view of the world based on the Bible looked like and how it explained humanity's situation and God's response to it. Light bulbs began to go off in my mind as they gave bible-based explanations that accurately described and matched the reality of what I had learned about human history, had observed in the lives of people, and had experienced in my own life. They described the life, death, and resurrection of Jesus and how He made it possible to be right with God in a way that was clearly impossible for anyone to obtain through their own efforts. They said that even if we had prayed to accept Jesus as Lord and Savior before, we should con-sider doing it again, and they would be glad to lead us.

It's hard to describe, but suddenly, everything made sense to me, and I knew that I needed to follow their lead and embrace what they said in the prayer. At that moment I had absolute confidence that God had been relentlessly pursuing me. It was like He had actually hunted me down and maneuvered me into a corner that had a door on each wall. I knew that I could go through the one door and keep on living my life as I had been and suffer the consequences of doing so. Or I could go through the door that He had been revealing to me in so many ways over the months. But I knew that if I chose that door, I had to go through it on my knees in surrender to the rule and reign of Jesus over my life.

It felt like their invitation to pray was Jesus saying to me that I needed to not just receive what He'd done on the cross to make me right with God, but that I also needed to fully submit my life to His design for me from that day forward. It was painfully obvious that if I didn't bow to Him right then, I would be making the biggest of the many mistakes of my life until that moment. When they told us to close our eyes and repeat what they said, but directly to God, I humbly but confidently bowed to Him with my heart, spirit, and mind, and committed myself to serve Him the rest of my life in whatever way He directed. When the leader finished the prayer and we all opened our eyes, he told us that we were now new creations in Christ, true children of God and members of His family, and the brothers and sisters of everyone else who had also surrendered to the rule and reign of Jesus over their lives.

Church member, employee, manager

After attending for a couple of months, we sensed that God was leading us to find a smaller church. We had received a flyer in the mail promoting a fairly new evangelical church that met at a local elementary school. On our first day there, the pastor and thirty or so other members embraced us in a way that we had never experienced before. We loved it, and as soon as we got into the car with the kids after the service, we knew we had found our church home. And you guessed it, another identity itch had been scratched—we would consider ourselves as members of this small community of Jesus followers.

I couldn't fully grasp what it was, but I had this unnatural confidence that clarity would come as we immersed ourselves in the life of the church, and I pressed in to knowing Him at a deeper level through devouring what He had revealed about Himself in His written word. All I knew was that until I was given the key that would unlock the identity-related mysteries that I had both experienced and observed, I absolutely loved the fact that a group of people I had never met truly viewed me and related to me as a fellow child of God. They treated me as a brother who had both been adopted into His family just like they had been—willfully choosing to follow Jesus, and also longing to become more and more like Him.

A combination of our love for Jesus, our desire to become like Him, and the kindness and care that this beautiful group of people lavished upon us, coupled with the new truth we had learned that serving others was actually serving Him, moved us to volunteer to help with the children's ministry of our church. Our son had just turned five, and our daughter was almost four during our first few months attending. We had received the blessing of having other young married couples with their own children serve our kids in this role. We knew then that it was the time for us to take the same step. I was totally out of my comfort zone, but with Helen and her natural gifts with young children at my side, we jumped in with both feet.

Both of us were working full time, and I was still taking classes at the local community college, as we integrated into the life stream of our home church. I had continued to jump from one job to another. I went from being a stenographer in the San Diego County Tax Collector's office in the secured tax division, to an apprentice machinist at an aircraft-tool-making company. After that, I held an administrative position with a local plating company and had then been an advertising representative for a publishing company that produced two different magazines for agriculture-related audiences in San Diego County.

In April of 1981, about six months before we began attending the church, I had taken an evening and weekend job at a corporate-owned 7-Eleven store less than a mile from where we lived. I watched the kids until the afternoon each weekday and then took them to a babysitter for a couple of hours. Helen picked them up after she got off from her shift. I either went to work or went to class each weekday afternoon and evening, and then worked a full eight hours on Saturday and Sunday afternoons and evenings.

The variety of responsibilities that had to be accomplished to work successfully in a convenience store, including customer interaction, was exhilarating to me. Within a few months my shift supervisor had told my store manager how well I was doing. He asked me if I could do a few hours during the day shift a couple of times per week so he could begin training me for a supervisor position. It wasn't long before my shift supervisor left the company, and I was asked to step into his role.

A few months later, my store manager began telling our district representative about me and asked if I'd be willing to transfer to another store to train as that store's manager. He told me up front that it was a store that had employee morale problems, serious inventory issues, and a poor track record for producing accurate administrative reports to the district office, and that none of the other existing store managers wanted to take it on.

The date they requested me to transfer would be during a semester break, so I was able to accept the position and switch to taking classes on weeknights. It created a number of childcare challenges for us, but the substantial pay raise was more than enough to cover costs and to also provide a little breathing room in our monthly budget. We quickly fell into a work, church, and night school rhythm as a family and sensed that we were right where God designed for us to be at that season of our lives.

Less than a month after being trained at that store, my trainer abruptly resigned, and I was installed as the store manager. I had just turned twenty-three years old. I loved being in the driver's seat and being responsible for every facet of managing the store but also having the freedom to change the way things were being done to accomplish the end goal. I experienced a level of exhilaration and satisfaction like never before, and I loved it. I was able to quickly turn the store around in every area, and after four months, my district manager asked me to move to another store having similar problems to try to turn it around too. As much as I loved the way my first store was humming along, I didn't want to pass up the opportunity to test my ability to do it again, so I accepted the transfer and took over another store in town.

A few weeks after I arrived at the next broken store, the district manager said that he thought I had a promising future in the business and said that he wanted to send me through the Certified Store Manager course. At that time, Southland corporation owned almost fifteen stores in San Diego County (about twice that number were franchises), and they only offered the course to a few of their best store managers. I accepted the challenge, went through the four-month program, and became a Certified Store Manager. Once I was certified, they asked me to take over another store that also had problems but not nearly like the other two I had stepped into. But this one was different. It was the highest-volume store in town, was the only one that sold gasoline, and had the highest number of employees.

While these things were happening in my work life, our church had made the move to an office building complex about two miles from where we had been meeting at the elementary school. Attendance began increasing, and the number of children we were teaching in our Sunday school class was also growing. I finished my associate's degree while managing the gas store and graduated in June of 1983. I had already developed a time schedule to complete my reading for my college classes, and since I was finished and had no plans to continue my education, I began devouring books on theology and evangelism and biographies of some great men and women of God.

As much as I loved the role of being a convenience store manager, the five and a half day, fifty-four-hours-per-week schedule, along with the constant challenge of finding and keeping a good midnight shift employee and the company's ongoing efforts to fight both customer and employee theft from store inventory, made it increasingly difficult to envision staying with the company for an extended period of time. Eventually, I made the difficult decision to resign from a job that I loved and that I had become convinced could have been my career for the rest of my life.

A few days after I resigned, I took a job as a fire watch through the laborer's union at the nuclear power plant about forty miles from where we lived. It was a good hourly wage, which is one reason why I took it. The other was the fact that I knew my brain wouldn't need to be engaged too deeply, which would make it possible for me to think about and memorize Bible verses. That plan totally bombed. I tried to keep my brain engaged while I sat or stood next to a fire extinguisher and watched plumbers, pipe fitters, and iron workers welding or grinding, but I just couldn't do it. Every hour seemed like a week, and I was totally miserable.

After the second full week, all the fire watchers were called into a meeting and informed that a percentage of us would be laid off. As soon as the meeting was over, I approached my foreman and volunteered to be part of the layoff. He looked at me like I was nuts, but I knew if I didn't get out of there, preferably in an honorable way, I actually would go bonkers and be tempted to just up and quit. He gave me the layoff paperwork at the end of the shift, and I was tempted to dance all the way out to my car. I was more than ready, and very excited, to begin looking for a new job bright and early on Monday morning.

That weekend went great, church was awesome (as usual), and the job search began at the start of the new week. I called a number of listings in the help-wanted section of the newspaper. One posting was for a route driver position with a uniform company in the National City area of San Diego. I was told over the phone to visit their plant and fill out an application. I made the twenty-five-mile drive as soon as I hung up the phone, filled out the application, and then turned around and drove the twenty-five miles back to Escondido.

They called me the next day and asked me to come in for an interview. When I arrived, I took a seat in the lobby alongside about ten other people who were also there for an interview. When my turn came, the general manager asked me a variety of questions, told me about the company and what he expected out of his employees, and then told me if I was a part of the final selection group, they would call me. They did, and I went from being a part of a group of sixty candidates, to a group of six. I was interviewed by the route supervisor and a few days later, got the call telling me that I was in the final four. This meant that I would spend a day with one of their existing drivers, riding around with him, and seeing what the job really entailed.

A couple of days later they called me once again, told me the job was mine, guided me through the steps I needed to take to register with the local Teamster's union, and told me to come to work the following Monday for orientation and training. The first Monday in July of 1983, I officially became a route driver for the Unitog uniform and supply company. Right from the start, I was making more money than I had when I was managing 7-Elevens and had a great benefits package, being part of the union.

I was given my own route within thirty days of my start date, and I loved it. I drove a UPS type of delivery truck and visited about ninety-five different businesses each week, scattered around the different cities of the southern part of San Diego County. I built some great friendships with the owners, managers, and many of the workers at each stop. I also told many of them that I was a Christian, and that if they needed prayer for anything, I would be happy to go to God on their behalf. When they heard that, dozens of them began opening up to me and asking me to pray for whatever was going on in their lives. I faithfully lifted them and their concerns to my heavenly Father.

Pastoring, an unsought calling

My brother had joined the army the previous year and had been stationed with his family at Ft. Bragg in North Carolina. A couple of months after I began working as a route driver, he and his wife called me one evening and started by telling me that they had begun attending a Southern Baptist church in the city just outside the base. They said the church had given the members that were interested an opportunity to take some sort of ministry-gift test. They explained they took the test for me based on what they knew about me, and that the test revealed to them that God has blessed me with the gifts needed to be a pastor.

What they said caught me completely off guard. I told them that if I could do anything I wanted as a career for the rest of my life, I wanted to host a radio talk show and be a writer. I said that being in vocational ministry as a pastor wasn't something I had ever considered and thus wasn't even on my radar. They were quick to point out that they were simply sharing their perspective about me and that I shouldn't take it as some kind of revelation given to them by God for me. They wanted me to know because they wanted to bless and encourage me.

At that point, I really was growing in my relationship with God, my understanding of His word, what His original design for life actually was, and in my desire to represent Him properly to everyone I came in contact with (especially those that didn't yet know Him in my workplace and neighborhood). I definitely wasn't thinking of living that way for Him from within the realm of vocational ministry. When I hung up the phone after our conversation, I told Helen what they had said and then just placed it in the "gee whiz" file in my mind and kept moving.

It wasn't long after that when quite a few people in the church began telling me how simply I explained complex spiritual truths that they had never fully grasped before then.

They remarked about how I seemed to have a really good grasp of the Bible even though I was young in age and still young in Jesus. With all of this buzz going on, my pastor asked me to fill in one night as the teacher of a home Bible study group of twenty church members who were all over the age of fifty.

Two of the church elders attended the group, and they wanted me to put into practice the teaching gift that they were fairly convinced God had given me. As soon as they asked me, the words of my brother and his wife were resurrected in my mind, and I sensed I was being moved down a path toward a destination that was very different, and much bigger in its ramifications, than I had ever imagined. With the feedback I received after I taught that Bible study, I began permitting my ever-active mind to run with the idea that God might truly be calling me into a pastoral ministry vocation.

A few weeks later, our pastor invited one of his friends to teach at our church's Sunday-morning services. This brother had recently moved his family from a small town in Northern Washington to Manila, Philippines, to start a church in the Asian megacity. The story he told of how God had orchestrated his move from public school teaching into full-time pastoral ministry, and then to uproot his family and move to the other side of the world, had me hanging on every word.

By the time he began describing the incredible need for healthy, Bible-based churches in another country, and the apparent openness of the people who lived there, I had fully embraced the idea that God was not only calling me to be a pastor, but more than likely, to exercise that gift somewhere beyond the borders of the United States at some point in the near future. Less than a week later I purchased and began reading the first of dozens of missionary biographies that I have read over the years.

While all of this was stirring in my personal, family, and church life, I was in such good momentum at work that I wound up receiving the Route Driver of the Month award twice within a time span of six months. But as much as I was enjoying and prospering financially in my job, it was becoming clear to me that God had been orchestrating all of the details and events in the various spheres of my life as preparation for another major transition. Although I didn't know exactly how or when He would move things forward, I was 100 percent convinced that He would.

I continued to devour missionary biographies and spend time with vacationing or former missionaries on weeknights or weekends and serve within the church. In early1985, I had the blessing of playing a significant role in sending out the first missionary family from our somewhat larger, but still relatively small, local church. Walking with them through their journey to the mission field, and then serving them in various ways, moved my wife and me to seriously ask God whether He could use people like us to be part of His work around the world.

Through a variety of God-guided circumstances that took place throughout the first half of that year, I was invited to join the church staff as an assistant pastor. I resigned from my job the first week of December, 1985, and began working for the church the following week. I wasn't sure how, but I was confident that job had proven to be exactly what He knew I needed to ensure that my life inventory was stocked perfectly for the next season of my life that He had designed for me. As happy and encouraging as my pastor, the elders, and most of the members of the church were when I joined the church staff as the assistant pastor, they also knew that God had been stirring up a passion in my heart to serve Him on the mission field and that more than likely, serving them full time would be short.

CHAPTER SIX

Advocate for the Disabled (1986)

Abandoning a "widget" mindset

Going from the workplace into "ministry" was a more difficult transition than I expected. In the workplace—at least in the industries that I'd always worked in—productivity could be measured, and thus success was fairly easy to define. The ministry didn't operate that way. On my first day, I spent the whole morning talking with my pastor and praying. As I returned to my desk around noon, I had a thousand thoughts running through my mind. I was eager to both serve the members of our church and anxious to find ways to engage in serving our local community, with a goal of representing Jesus so well that they'd be open to me telling them the truths of the Gospel.

Everything I was doing day to day was very new to me that first week, so the whole production mentality that I'd always navigated by hadn't really created any stress for me. But by the middle of the second week, I began to feel like I had figured out the rhythm of being on the church staff, and I began wrestling with whether I was being productive enough to justify the salary I was receiving. My pastor recognized something was bothering me, and one day after our morning time of prayer, he told me to grab a cup of coffee and join him in his office.

He asked me how I was feeling about things and whether anything was bothering me. I told him I was struggling with whether or not I was being productive enough. After probing around with a few questions, he told me a key principle about pastoral ministry that I had never heard before. Put as succinctly as possible, he said that he knew I'd come to this point of struggle when he hired me, and that he had waited to explain because if he had told me about it before I actually experienced it, I probably wouldn't have given it the weight it deserved.

He said that most of the work world operated with a production mentality, and because of that, the primary measurement of success was how many "widgets" you designed, produced, sold, or serviced. Pastoral ministry wasn't like that because our primary responsibility was people work, not production work, and people work is almost impossible to measure. He went on to say that I was on staff as his assistant pastor because God had gifted and called me, and that I didn't have to justify my position by producing anything. He emphasized that this wasn't in any way, shape, or form a widget-based position. He basically ordered me to relax, seek the Lord, serve in the areas I'd been assigned, and to trust that I was right where God wanted me to be and that His hand was on me.

That talk completely lifted me out of the mental framework that I had fallen into, and within a week or so, my mindset began to change. I became more and more comfortable with the idea that I could read during the daytime, that time spent reading was a part of my job and would make me a better tool in God's hands. At the same time, I grew in confidence that I could be flexible with my schedule in order to do the "people" work that was caring for the members of the church. There was no reason for anyone to take time off from work to meet with me. I could meet at the location and time that was most convenient for them, whether it was before they went to work in the mornings, during their lunch breaks, or during the evenings.

Engaging the world of the disabled

Within a few weeks of that talk with my pastor, God opened the door for me to become involved in a ministry that would change my life forever. It began when I answered the church phone one afternoon. The woman on the line told me that her son, who had cerebral palsy, had just been moved from Los Angeles to a new home for the disabled in our area. She said that it had a unique layout on beautiful grounds and that they were doing some cutting-edge things in caring for people with disabilities.

She explained that her son was a Bible-believing Christian in his late twenties, and he wanted to have a pastor come and visit him. She also said that he wanted to talk about the idea of starting a weekly Bible study on the premises for him and other interested residents to attend. Since I had been asking God to not only help me serve the members of our church but to also engage our local community, I received this as a possible answer to my prayer. I wrote down her details and told her I would visit her son the next day.

Up until that point in my life, I hadn't really been exposed to people with disabilities, and I knew nothing about cerebral palsy in particular. I was confident that if God wanted me to walk through this door, He would give me the understanding and everything else necessary to be the blessing I desired to be. As I pulled into the complex the next afternoon, I was quite impressed. There were a number of beautiful homes, single level, and side by side. Each building had a nice sign with a name on it, and there were disabled people buzzing about in their electric wheelchairs, going from one house to another or to and from the administration building. On the right was a much larger house that also had a name on it. As soon as I walked through the door of the administration building, the receptionist greeted me with a smile and asked how she could help me. I introduced myself and told her whom I was there to see, and that my visit was in response to his mother's call. She gave me directions to his home, and I walked over to that building.

The door was propped open as I approached, and the first thing I noticed was how wide the doorway was. Clearly, the buildings had been designed and built for people in wheelchairs. As I entered, I passed another doorway on my left as I moved toward the living room area ahead. I glanced in that room as I passed it and saw a number of empty electric wheelchairs sitting side by side, each of them connected by cords to wall sockets. There was also a computer sitting on a desk, and although it looked crowded, the room was very organized. The living room area was furnished with a couch, a stuffed chair, a coffee table, and a TV. A man in a wheelchair was watching the TV. He looked up when he noticed me, and I greeted him. He gave me a big smile but didn't say anything.

Just then, a young man walked out of the kitchen in response to hearing me greet the man watching the TV. He welcomed me, introduced himself, and said that he was the caregiver assigned to the six residents who lived in this three-bedroom house. I, in turn, introduced myself, told him whom I was there to visit, and that I had come in response to the request of the resident's mother. He seemed genuinely happy that I was there to see the young man. He guided me through the living room to a hallway. We passed a huge disability-equipped bathroom before walking through the second bedroom door on the right.

When we entered the room, the young man I was there to see, DJ, turned to look at us. He raised his eyebrows, smiled as well as he could, and groaned joyfully. He had dark, black hair and a carefully trimmed mustache. Two seat-belt-like straps held him in his chair. One was around his waist and the other around his chest. His legs were straight and stiff out in front of him, resting on an extension that jutted out from the seat. His arms were bent and stiff, and so were his hands. The only nonpainful movement he could make was with his neck and his eyebrows. He did have some control of his jaw, but his mouth was almost always open with his tongue hanging out just a bit, which caused his saliva to flow fairly freely.

Over the arms of the wheelchair, almost like the food-holding table portion of a high chair, was a large wooden board sitting across his lap. This board was his communication device. It was covered with crate paper that had numbered columns across the top and letters, words, and phrases listed in each column. The whole thing was covered with Plexiglas and, although it was very scratched in places, it was still serving its essential purpose.

The aide introduced me to DJ and then asked me if I had ever communicated with a board like this before. I told him that I hadn't, and so he demonstrated how to use it. Beginning with the first column heading on the left, he pointed with his finger to the number at the top of the column and then looked at DJ. He said, "One, two, three, four," and as soon as he said "four" DJ looked up at him, somewhat winking. Then, he proceeded down column number four pointing at each word, and after the fifth word, DJ looked up at him again and winked. This was the first word of the sentence. He spoke the word to DJ and asked him if it was right, and DJ raised his eyebrows. Then he started again with the numbers at the top of each column and repeated the process. I had never considered how someone unable to write or speak might communicate with others, so I was mesmerized at what I was seeing take place before me. At the same time, though, I recognized that an enormous amount of time was required to have a conversation composed of more than two or three sentences. The aide then told me that he needed to get back to preparing dinner and left me there to get to know DJ.

His mom had told me on the phone that his IQ was at a genius level, so I knew before I sat down to talk with him that he was actually smarter than I was. But now that I was face to face with him and talking to him using his board, I had to fight my natural instinct to talk to him using language as if he were a child. Clearly, he could think and read, and he desperately wanted to communicate. But he lived in a constant state of frustration generated by the reality that anyone who looked at him probably assumed that he was as disabled mentally as he was physically, and that only a few of them had the time or patience necessary to have a meaningful conversation with him in order to discover that wasn't true.

After telling him about his mom's call, I shared some of my story and then asked him how he liked this new place that was now his home. He said he liked it and was happy to be there. He also said that he would like for me to visit him as often as possible. He then told me that he really wanted to have someone come and teach a Bible study there and that if I started one, there were many other residents who would also attend. I told him that I would pray about it, speak with my pastor to see what he thought, and then make a trip back to let him know if I was going to be able to make it happen.

After I said goodbye, I walked back to my car, got in and shut the door, and then just sat there for fifteen minutes or so trying to process what I had just experienced. I was a mixed bag of thoughts and emotions. I knew that my visit had been a huge blessing to a newfound brother in Jesus and that God's plan was for our relationship to deepen. But at the same time, the fact that I had to consciously fight the urge to not treat him like a child, and that I felt awkward and embarrassed each time that I needed to wipe the drool from his chin while we talked, gnawed at me.

A God-given special friend

I spoke with my pastor the next morning, and he told me the opportunity sounded like an answer to prayer and that I should go for it. On Monday morning, after telling Helen and others about this door that I was convinced God had opened and asking them to pray, I went back to the facility to tell DJ the good news. As I entered the living room area of the home, DJ was sitting in his chair facing in my direction, while another man in a chair with his back toward me was talking to him using very articulate speech. When he saw me, DJ looked up, got a big smile on his face, and grunted. The other man swiveled his chair around and greeted me. He asked me if I was the pastor that DJ had been telling him about. I said that I was, and I introduced myself as he extended his arm and hand as best as he could to shake my hand. As I gently grasped his stiff fingers in my hand, he told me his name was Matt, that he was a Christian too, and that he was a good friend of DJ's.

I walked over and gently squeezed DJ's shoulder and asked him how he was doing. I grabbed a chair and sat down with the two of them. Matt was in his early thirties, had crew-cut brown hair, and was clean shaven. His left eye drifted in different directions while he focused on you with his right eye, and as I'd already learned, he was able to speak very clearly. He had full control of his neck, mouth, tongue, and jaw muscles. His upper torso was about the same size as mine, and he had almost full control of his shoulder muscles and elbow muscles. His wrists, hands, and fingers were stiff, but he was able to move the knob on his electric wheelchair and thus be independent and mobile. His hip sockets were totally stiff and locked in place, as were the muscles in his legs, which had shrunken up, almost into a fetal position. He had a specially designed form on the backrest and seat of his wheelchair that made it possible for him to sit upright and relieve as much pressure from his hip sockets as possible.

As soon as we had introduced ourselves, DJ grunted, and Matt turned back to him. Matt then started reciting the numbers at the top of the columns on DJ's board. He grunted at column six and then, without looking, Matt began reciting, in order, the words and phrases that were in that column. I couldn't believe it. He had memorized DJ's board. I was amazed as I watched Matt communicate with DJ. He'd get a whole sentence out of DJ in less than a minute, and there were even times that he'd finish a sentence before DJ had given him all the words. It was fascinating to watch and something I'll never forget.

Eventually, I told the two of them that I had been given approval for the Bible study and if they would set it up within the time parameters I gave them, we could start as soon as they were ready. DJ grinned and grunted; he was so excited. Matt told me that he knew quite a few people who would attend and that he, of course, would be there too. Before I left, I asked Matt if I could return and spend some time alone with him to really get to know him, and he said he'd be happy to.

I did meet with Matt alone a few days later and learned his life story. At the time our friendship began, both of his parents had already passed away, and the only family he had was his older brother, who lived in the LA area. Matt was a solid Christian, understood biblical principles, and felt like God wanted to use him in the ministry. What became apparent to me, but what he never really embraced, was that God was *already* using him incredibly in the lives of the people who lived at Mountain Shadows. I say that because I discovered over the next few months that he had memorized the boards of many of the other residents. Whenever he was on the property, he regularly went from house to house to spend time with those who were nonverbal. His visit with them was probably the only form of conversation most of them had had that day.

Matt had a gift, and an anointing, and although he never fully saw it at the level he probably should have, he was the onsite shepherd that God had provided for this unique group of people. Because of the challenges with his eyes, he struggled to read and had discovered that, by nature or by necessity, he was an oral learner. His heart longed to go to Bible college and actually study the Word in a classroom setting. He told me that he had friends who were looking into registering at a Bible school that was hosted by a local church, and eventually he wound up attending that school. Once he began as a student there, I was able to help him study, from time to time, for some of the classes he was taking.

He had a sneaky and quirky sense of humor that I experienced for the first time not long after I got to know him. Although he actually left the Mountain Shadows complex on a regular basis, because he worked a few hours each day at the United Cerebral Palsy center across town, he always had to ride the special bus for the disabled back and forth. While he was there, he was working in a room with only a few nondisabled people. The majority of his coworkers also had CP. Compared to the others at Mountain Shadows who weren't as high functioning as Matt was, his world was much larger than theirs, but compared to our world, there was no comparison.

An unforgettable dinner

The more I spoke with Matt and got to know him, the more I recognized that he loved to eat as much as I did. I could also tell that he would seize any opportunity to get out of Mountain Shadows, by way of any type of transportation, and into the larger community where fully functional people lived. One day, while I was meeting with him at Mountain Shadows, I told him I'd take him out to the restaurant of his choice for dinner. He said he loved pizza and that he especially loved Round Table pizza, so I told him that I'd be back the next afternoon to pick him up to grab some pizza together. I also asked him if he could feed himself, and he told me that wouldn't be a problem.

The next day, I had my first lesson on how to load this heavy guy into the passenger seat of my car. Believe me, it wasn't easy. Because his hips and tightened-up legs were frozen stiff pointing to the left, I had to put them in to the car first and then follow them in with his upper torso and shoulders. The problem was that I'm right handed, and so my right arm, my strongest arm, was cradling his shrunken legs, the lightest part of his body. This meant that I had to put my left arm across his back and under his left armpit, making my weakest arm responsible for the bulk of his weight. Coupled with the fact that I'm six feet, three inches tall and needed to hunch over to actually get him in, it's fairly easy to grasp how difficult it was to transport him. It didn't help that he weighed about 140 pounds, the majority of which was above his waist.

He grimaced and grunted in obvious pain as I put his legs in the car and then tilted him upright with his back into the seat. He was still groaning as I tried to pull the seat belt over him, and he told me through clenched teeth to wait on the seat belt because he needed to be repositioned in the seat since his hips and legs were killing him. I asked him how to do it. He instructed me to lean over in front of him with my right hand under his left armpit and my left hand under his right armpit, then lift him up while pushing him back deeper into the seat. To gain enough leverage to do so, I had to put my right leg in through the door and over the top of his legs. By God's grace, I was able to get it done, and the pressure on his legs was relieved. He chuckled as his voice went back to normal, and I belted him in.

I folded up his nonelectric wheelchair and stuffed it into my trunk, and off we went. Once we arrived at the parking lot of the restaurant, I unloaded his chair, brought it around to the passenger door and then asked him how to get him out. He said this one would be easy. I could just grab him under his armpits and lift his upper body out, and his feet would follow. I followed his instructions, and it went much easier than loading him in the car earlier. I then wheeled him to the door of the restaurant and left him just far enough back so that when I opened the door it would clear him, but close enough so that I could race back around behind his chair and push it through before the door closed automatically. I was already beginning to understand why very few people would come and pick up residents from Mountain Shadows and take them out to different places. It took planning, physical strength, and plenty of time. Then, as with entering the door to the restaurant, you had to think about things you didn't normally need to when navigating day to day without disabilities.

I moved a chair aside and pushed Matt's wheelchair up to the table until its armrests came in contact with the edge of the table. There were only two booths and one other table occupied in the restaurant at the time we arrived, and I noticed immediately that the kids at one of the booths were watching us. The parents glanced over nonchalantly but kept on talking to each other while the kids, being kids, kept staring. Matt told me the kind of pizza he liked and the kind of soda he wanted, and I went up to order.

I brought our drinks back and asked him what the best way was for him to drink comfortably. He asked me to put a straw in the drink and then hold the glass up next to the side of his face, making sure the straw went into the left corner of his mouth. As soon as I had it in there correctly, he clamped his lips down around the straw, closed his mouth and drank a few swallows. Some of it went down his windpipe, and he started to cough, and although he had drunk down most of it, there was enough left to come bursting back out like a fountain. He couldn't cover his mouth because of the condition of his arms and hands, and so each time he coughed, liquid droplets were launched over our table. Because it sounded like he was choking, and the sound wasn't muffled by his hand, everyone in the restaurant began staring at us with concern, checking to see if he was okay. After his windpipe was cleared, he stopped coughing and started laughing. He had one of the coolest laughs I'd ever heard. He explained to me that he did that regularly when eating or drinking, and that it was no big deal. Everyone in the restaurant went back to their meals and conversations, but the kids at that one table kept right on watching.

We talked for a bit more until our number was called and our pizza was ready. When I got back to the table, I asked him what I needed to do to help him eat. A sneaky grin came over his face as he told me that it would be best if I cut it up and fed it to him. I knew immediately that I had been duped by him! He had told me that he could feed himself, and I had seen him at his house clutching a piece of bread between his stiff fingers and getting it back and forth to his mouth. So, I was surprised when he told me to cut it up and feed it to him and asked him why he told me he could feed himself if he really couldn't. He said that he could but that the pizza would be hot on his fingers, that it would sag and the topping would fall off, and that he was starving and it would take way too long to feed himself. His grin expanded as he looked at me with that look in his eyes that communicated, "I gotcha, and I'm happy I did." He seemed overjoyed at my having to do something that would take me out of my comfort zone because it gave me a taste of what he went through on a day-to-day basis.

A glimpse of what was in me

As we continued our meal, I strongly sensed that God was in the midst of this relationship and that this whole trip and dinner with Matt was by His design and not primarily for Matt's good, but for mine. I knew that He was knocking off some edges I had that needed to be done away with for further usefulness to Him. Although I knew all of this, I still felt a tinge of what I would call embarrassment, for lack of a better term, as I put the first forkful of pizza into Matt's mouth. Once he had taken it off the fork, he leaned his head back and started chewing with his mouth open most of the time. Apparently, he had sinus problems on a regular basis and couldn't breathe too well out of his nose. He swallowed the first bite quickly and was ready for another one. I took a quick bite for myself and then cut up another piece for him and placed it up to his mouth. This time, something got caught in his windpipe, and he started to choke again. But, as you can imagine, it wasn't just liquid droplets flying out of his mouth. He was spewing partially chewed pieces of pizza all over the table. Again, everyone looked at us, and again he was fine within a minute or so and asked me for another bite.

It's hard to put into words what I was feeling during that dinner with Matt. We ate the whole pizza and talked a lot, and I enjoyed the time with him. Yet the looks from the people in the restaurant made me feel uncomfortable. It seemed like they were communicating with their looks and facial expressions that we were disrupting their dining experience. It felt to me like they were nonverbally berating us to just stay home, and that they were uncomfortable, or we distracted them from their nice evening out. I may have been reading too much into it, but that is what I really felt.

One of the reasons I thought this of them was because I found myself feeling very uncomfortable by having to feed Matt in the first place and even more uneasy each time he coughed and launched a portion of the contents of his mouth into the air and then down onto his chest, my arm, and the table. Plainly put, I was embarrassed. I felt like I was responsible for intruding on the comfortable world of the other patrons' dining experience. I really did feel that way, yet the more embarrassed I felt, the more convicted I felt by the Holy Spirit that my embarrassment was nothing more than selfish pride.

I couldn't fully get a mental handle on it or understand the lesson that God wanted me to learn from all of this. Another incident with Matt many years later gave me an even clearer picture of what God had begun to show me about myself that evening at the pizza restaurant.

We wound up dining there for about an hour and a half, and then I began the process of loading him back into my car to take him back to Mountain Shadows. It was an awesome time together, and I knew that God had given me a special relationship with Matt, a relationship that would glorify Him by our getting to know and loving one another.

CHAPTER SEVEN
Missionary (1986–1993)

A dream from God about another child

About a month before I joined the staff of the church, I had a very vivid dream about Helen becoming pregnant again and having another boy, whom we named Matthew Elijah. It was the most real dream that I'd ever had. The fact that I remembered it in such detail after I woke up convinced me that it just might be God telling us that we should have another child and that it would probably be a boy. If we did get pregnant again, and she did have another boy, then clearly, we would name him Matthew Elijah.

Prior to that day, we were totally content with having a son and a daughter and had no plans for adding another child to our family. That morning, when I shared the dream with Helen and that I thought it might have been God revealing what He wanted us to do, it caught her totally off guard. She said she was open to the idea, but that we needed to really think and pray about it for a few days before making the decision to do what was necessary for her be pregnant again. We did pray, and even though she wasn't as confident that it was a God-sent notion as I was, she agreed to move forward with the plan.

A miraculous answer to prayer

My pastor, whom I was becoming familiar with as my "boss," informed me that he wanted me to not only serve our own church and community, but to be prepared for the possibility of God calling me and my family to become missionaries. He encouraged me and gave me the time to meet during the week with vacationing missionaries, to attend missionary-related training courses, and to research and build a missionary-sending structure within our church. If God was going to call us to be missionaries, it would launch our family first and then the others he believed God would send to the mission field after us.

As Helen and I discussed the possibility of God calling us to move overseas, we both felt like one major confirmation would be God providing the finances for me in some way to make a short visit to whatever place He might command us to go. To be on the church staff, I had accepted a salary that was less than half of what I was making as a route driver who was a member of a union. This meant that we had absolutely no money available that could be used to pay for a trip that we knew would cost us more than $1,000.

Through the missionary our church had sent to Guam just more than a year before, I came to know about an existing church on one of the Marshall Islands needing a pastor. The correspondence with the church leaders over there sounded promising at first, but it became apparent that I wouldn't have been a good fit for them, and vice versa. We kept praying, and I kept inquiring.

In March of 1986, my pastor decided to pay a personal visit to the missionaries we had sent to Guam. He told me he wanted me to teach both Sunday-morning and evening services while he was gone. The week before he left, however, we discovered that Helen was pregnant with the child that my dream had moved us to try to conceive. The due date for this baby, who we thought could very well be our second son and whom we already had a name for, was the third week of September.

At the helm of the church in my pastor's absence, I didn't have any time to continue inquiring about possible places of need overseas. But while I was in that phase of not seeking out opportunities, Helen and I continued to ask God to confirm whether being missionaries was His will for us by providing the resources for me to afford a visit to another country. It was in that short season of not actively seeking a place to go but continuing in prayer for God to provide and guide that He responded.

When I had finished praying at the conclusion of the Sunday evening Bible study the first weekend our pastor was gone, a member of our church from the Philippines approached me after the service. Her husband had passed away four months earlier on the day after Christmas. We had become very close with them and their daughter, who was the same age as Travis. Helen and I had spent quite a bit of time trying to comfort her and her daughter in the midst of their grieving, and our connection became tighter than it had ever been.

She faithfully attended every church service, and I loved seeing her in the audience with her Bible open and taking notes on my messages. That night, I noticed that she was waiting for me to finish praying with someone so she could speak with me. When she walked up, she said that she had been praying for God's plan for our family, and He had revealed to her that He had something for us to accomplish in her home country—and that she wanted to pay for a round-trip ticket for me to go and discover what it was.

Needless to say, I was caught completely off guard by her words. She knew she had just completely blown me away, and as I thought through how I should respond, she gave me the rest of the details. She was going to purchase tickets for her and her daughter to fly to Manila near the end of June, and if I wanted to go, I could accompany them on the flight to Manila and return back to the US at the time of my choosing, after I had seen whatever God intended for me to see. After answering a few questions that immediately popped into my mind, she told me that if I did want to go, I needed to apply for a passport as soon as possible.

I don't remember why, but Helen had stayed home with the kids that night. On the drive home, I had some time to think about what had just happened. I had a powerful sense of awe at God's goodness, while also being overcome with shame at the reality that although

I had been praying for something like this to happen, but in my heart of hearts, I really didn't believe that it would actually become a reality. When I got home, I sat Helen down on the couch and told her I had some big news for her. She was visibly stunned upon hearing, and tears welled up in her eyes.

We both knew that my natural inclination would be to take the initiative to approach this woman for further confirmation, but we decided that if it was really God stirring this woman, He would move her to reapproach us about it. The following weekend, just before the start of the first Sunday-morning service, she walked up to me again and said that if I wanted to go, I needed to give her my full name and the specific day I'd like to return to the States, so she could move forward with purchasing the tickets.

I had spent the whole week praying and thinking about the trip, wondering which specific locations God wanted me to visit. Every prayer included a plea for Him to speak to me when I was in the location He wanted my family and me to move to as missionaries. I remembered that the missionary pastor who spoke to our church the previous year had mentioned the need for a Bible-teaching church in the second-largest city in the country. It was called Cebu City and was about four hundred miles south of Manila on the island of Cebu, which sat in the middle of many of the other smaller islands, known as the Visayas, which comprise the central part of the country.

The last week of June in 1986, I flew with her and her daughter to Manila and spent the first three days with their family in the small town where she grew up, about three hours from Manila. After returning to Manila, the plan was for this woman, and the pastor of our sister church there, to fly with me to Cebu City to check things out. Our flight was scheduled for late afternoon, but on the morning of that day, both of them called me at the church office where I had been staying and said they couldn't make the trip.

By that time, I was so convinced God wanted me to visit Cebu City that I decided I would make the trip alone. A woman who had been attending the church in Manila was in the office at the time I received those calls and heard my side of the phone conversations with them. She asked me what city I was planning on flying to that afternoon. I told her, and her eyes lit up. She said that she was born and raised in Cebu City and that she was flying there that afternoon too—on the same flight I would be on. The awe that both of us felt in God's orchestration of all this was amplified even more when I told her the reason I was going there.

She said she would be my guide to the city, and that's exactly what she did. After arriving at the airport, she rode with me in a taxi and helped me check into a very nice hotel. Two days later, after making a side trip to the next island over to meet a missionary and attend one of the services of his church, I returned to Cebu City. She met me in front of the university she had attended years before and then took me around the city, introducing me to old friends who were working in the downtown area.

The next day, sensing that I needed to feel the city on my own, I decided to take a taxi back to the heart of the city and prayerfully walk down the oldest and most famous street in a city that now contained almost two million people. As I stepped off the curb at the busiest intersection of that street, God silently but powerfully spoke to my spirit in a way I had never experienced before. He said this was the place He wanted me to bring my family to live out our faith in Him, draw people to Him, and pioneer a church that would faithfully teach His word. That moment is still etched in my mind. Whenever I think about it, I can still see crowds of people stepping off the curb with me to cross the street, smell the diesel fumes from the jeepneys, hear the cacophony of honking horns, and feel the sweaty and sticky feeling on my skin due to the heat and humidity.

Even though God had spoken so powerfully to me, I didn't call Helen to tell her when I got back to the hotel. Long-distance calls were so expensive that the plan was to wait to call her until I was back in Manila on the day I was scheduled to fly back home. It took everything within me to not ignore our existing plan, but God made clear that I should stick with that plan and use the interim time to press even further into Him and begin praying for her to be open to His voice too. When I did speak with her, I kept it short and sweet. I revealed what I was convinced I heard Him say to me and then simply asked her to seek Him about the idea herself.

As confident as I was that it was the Lord that spoke to me—that it was not something I dreamed up and then said to myself on His behalf—I knew that He needed to confirm this calling to Helen and my pastor and the leaders of our church. As much as I was ready personally to move forward and put the plan together, I had learned from the missionary biographies I'd read and the hours I'd spent with missionaries that when God calls someone to do something that requires the level of sacrifice necessary to make a move like that, He almost always confirms it to a number of other people who also know and love the ones He is calling.

As soon as I arrived back home on the first week of July, I recounted all that had happened on the trip, especially that moment in downtown Cebu. Helen was in the sixth month of the pregnancy at the time, and although she was overwhelmed at the idea of taking a newborn baby overseas, she said she would continue to pray about it. A few days later, I told my pastor and church leaders, and the wait for confirmation began.

My pastor wisely encouraged me to completely reengage with life and the ministry I was doing prior to the trip. He knew me well enough to know that I was already formulating a plan, and that my natural inclination would be to try and push things forward using the manipulation skills that I had been trying to surrender to God's control. I plunged back into things and willfully chose to be patient while waiting on the Lord to confirm to Helen and the church leaders what He had already spoken to me.

It wasn't easy, but I was able to restrain myself from talking about God's desire to use us to share His love and truth with the people of Cebu City and how much I had learned about them and their history through my research. Helen's pregnancy helped keep my mind busy, and a little more than two months later, she went into labor. As her delivery date drew closer, we decided that we should pick a name for a girl, just in case my dream about a boy named Matthew Elijah might not have come from God. There was a girl in Travis's class whose name was Katie Joy, and as soon as he mentioned her, we knew that was the name we'd use if it turned out Helen was carrying a girl. And sure enough, a little more than two months later, during the third week of September, we were surprised to welcome His gift of a girl, not a boy. Katie Joy, not Matthew Elijah, joined our family that day.

A calling confirmed, a departure realized

The three months from Katie's birth to Christmas passed quickly, and the significant amount of prayer being offered to God by us and on our behalf continued. Near the end of January in 1987, Helen told me that God had moved on her heart, and she was willing to move forward in obedience to His calling on our lives to relocate to the Philippines. When I told our pastor and church leaders, they said God had also confirmed it to them a few weeks earlier, but they didn't want to say anything to me until they had heard it from Helen.

Knowing that I would begin planning the details of our departure as soon as possible after receiving confirmation, Helen said she'd like to wait until after we celebrated Katie's first birthday in September. As much as I didn't want to wait that long, I agreed, and no surprise at all to Helen, I booked our flights to Manila for September 26, 1987, five days after her first birthday.

In the months prior to that day, we sold almost everything we possessed, loaded up what remained into ten airline-acceptable boxes, and boarded a flight that took us almost eight thousand miles away from where we had been living in Southern California.

As that Korean Air 747 climbed up and away from LAX that night, I remembered that I had sworn to myself back in 1978, at the conclusion of my army duty in Japan, that I'd never leave America again. I looked at my wife and my nine-, eight-, and one-year-old children sitting next to us, and the reality of what I had gotten them into hit me like a ton of bricks: Had I really just willfully detached them from everyone and everything familiar to them? What kind of parent does that? Had I made a mistake? At that moment, God bestowed a previously unexperienced level of peace into my heart and made clear that He was pleased with us, that we were all in His hands, and that the kids would be fine with living out what He had in store for us on the other side of the world.

When Helen and the kids nodded off to sleep a few hours after takeoff, I began thinking about the reality that we were now missionaries. This new status in both our own eyes and the eyes of others who knew and loved us, scratched another identity itch and once again reinforced the bible-based truths I had come to believe about God's design for the only part of His creation He made in His image and likeness, humanity. Specifically, that He has hard-wired every person to have an identity as an individual and also as a member of a variety of groups. But it wasn't just that. It was also the reality that I had discovered and then seen validated time and again when a person voluntarily does something that requires an out-of-the-ordinary level of self-denial. That when they do, others will naturally begin identifying them as a member of a group of people that have made similar sacrifices and then bestow an increased level of honor upon them, regardless of whether the person desires it or not.

As uncomfortable as it was for us to have our friends and even people we didn't know identify us and honor us like that, I had come to believe that God has designed things to operate that way. I'd observed that the vast majority of the members of the military, firefighters, and cops didn't begin doing what they do so they could be identified as part of a group that others bestow honor upon, but that's what always happened. And I had become convinced that God has inserted into every person an inclination to both ascribe honor to those that act in a way that is considered honorable, and to identify them in a positive way as a member of a group that lives out self-sacrifice and self-denial for the good of others. This God-given honor-bestowing instinct will express itself whether the person it's bestowed upon receives it or not.

A beautiful season of life in the Philippines

Helen's only prior memory of the Philippines was the traumatic and bittersweet twelve hours we spent at Clark Air Base hospital almost ten years earlier, when the very real possibility of losing our firstborn engulfed us. But as the wheels of our jumbo jet touched down in Manila, both of us were convinced that as He brought both tears and blessing during our presence in the Philippines all those years ago, He was going to do the same thing this time. And that's exactly what He did.

We spent the first week in Manila, overwhelmed by the heat, humidity, rain, flooding, and massive jet lag produced by almost twenty hours spent in a plane and the fifteen-hour time difference from where we had been living. We flew south and spent almost three months living in Dumaguete City, which is on the island of Negros. A few days after Christmas, in 1987, we made the move to the island of Cebu and into a rented house on the outskirts of Cebu City.

During our time living in Dumaguete City, we learned some of the basics of Filipino culture, the socioeconomic system that most Filipinos lived life within, and how difficult it was to do many of the things that comprise day-to-day life. Heeding the counsel of both Filipinos and missionaries, we hired two college-aged Filipina cousins and brought them to Cebu with us to assist with the rigors of day-to-day life in a developing country. They shared one of the bedrooms in the house we had rented and were absolutely crucial in helping us learn how to live for the next five years. We couldn't afford a washing machine, so they washed our clothes by hand. They also taught Helen how to shop at the open market, cleaned the house, cooked most of our meals, and took care of the small patch of grass and the plants that grew inside the fence that went around the perimeter of our house.

We enrolled our oldest two children in the international school that sat alongside the road that we had to travel to get to the heart of Cebu City and the downtown area. The school was from kindergarten through the equivalent of seventh grade, with about five hundred students attending. Ninety percent of them were Filipinos from upper-class families, and all but three of the teachers were Filipinos who had graduated from the best universities in the country or abroad. About a dozen of the students were Americans, with the rest of the foreign students coming from Germany, the UK, China, or other Southeast Asian countries.

Our children developed some very close friendships with a few of their classmates and a few of the kids in the subdivision where we lived. All in all, they did very well academically and socially. Between their classmates, the kids in our neighborhood, and the children of the people who became part of our church, they learned how to develop meaningful relationships with people who spoke English as a second language and whose culture was fundamentally different than their own.

Once the kids began attending school and a basic pattern of life had been developed, I joined a gym in the downtown area to get some exercise and to get to know some locals, with the hope of being able to share the Gospel with them. I chose that specific gym because I had met the unmarried woman who owned it during the exploration trip I had taken in 1986. At the time, she was working within a government agency but told me that she had always wanted to start her own business. By the time we moved there, her gym had already been open for about six months. She had been very kind during that original visit, and I wanted to not only reconnect with her, but also help support her business.

Within a few months, I had gotten to know quite a few people, and when they learned I was a Bible teacher, they showed some interest in learning what the Bible teaches directly from its pages. I offered to pay a small sum for rent for using the gym on Sundays before it opened at noon, and she accepted the offer. I then invited the folks I met to attend, and a few of them obliged. The owner was firmly entrenched in the religion she was raised with but sat in and listened to me teach each week. Helen and I connected with her, so we began inviting her over to our home on a regular basis and were able to hear her life story. In mid-February of 1988, she became the first person to surrender her life to Jesus through our efforts to live for Him and to tell others about Him in Cebu City.

God sent us a few others who already knew Him but hadn't yet plugged in to a local Bible-teaching church. The owner also began sharing her newfound faith in Jesus and inviting many of her friends; and quite a few of them came to Jesus, too. Within about six months, the congregation had grown to about twenty-five adults. We outgrew the gym, and about a year after we started, we moved to another location about half a mile away. Approximately two years later, we relocated downtown to the oldest street in the city—the very same street I walked down in 1986, when God told me this was where He wanted us.

During those first few years, the passion I had to teach the Bible was given the opportunity to express itself to a much larger group of people outside our little church than the small number that were part of it. For almost one full year, I was teaching eleven different Bible studies each week, to a variety of people, in a number of different settings. I taught three times per week inside the second-largest prison in the country, at a rattan factory, in an insurance office, at a costume jewelry factory, and even in an extremely poverty-stricken squatter's community, composed of blind adults who lived there with their spouses and children. Once again, my pastor's wisdom displayed itself when he strongly recommended I cut back to teaching only the Bible studies that were most likely to directly support the establishment of the church we were there to pioneer. Although I didn't like doing it, I acted on his counsel and eventually cut back on everything but the church services and the prison Bible study.

A visit home and a season of challenges

After seventeen months in the field, we went on a nine-week family visit back to the States while the kids were on summer break in April and May of 1989. The reconnection with our families, friends, and other church members refreshed our souls. The level of respect and honor with which we were received by everyone was humbling and made us feel awkward at times, but we followed the advice of other seasoned missionaries and church leaders and tried to be gracious receivers. I thoroughly enjoyed the opportunities I had to personally describe what God was doing through us and in us to the individuals and churches that were praying for us and supporting us financially.

After we returned to Cebu and picked up with life and ministry, we entered into a season of tumultuous trials. We spent seven days locked down on our island as a result of a number of Philippine military officers, in both Manila and Cebu, working together trying to overthrow the government of President Corazon Aquino.

Then, during a three-day family visit to a large city on the island of Negros, just west of Cebu, our section of the country was pretty much demolished by a category-five typhoon. At the time it was actually pummeling the city where we were staying, I was lying on the floor of our hotel room with a very high fever and every muscle of my body screaming out with pain any time I moved. The hotel took some heavy damage from the storm, and the power to the whole region of the country was out for at least five days.

Our short flight back to Cebu was scheduled for the next day, but due to typhoon damage on both islands, it had to be canceled. My condition wasn't getting any better, so we decided that if we couldn't get a flight out the day after our original one, I would go and see a doctor there in the city of Bacolod. I was actually feeling worse the next day, but we were able to get a flight home, so I pushed through what I was feeling, and away we went. The airport for Cebu City is on a small island called Mactan that sits just off the eastern coast of the city. Other than transit through a variety of different-sized boats, the only way to cross the channel in a vehicle was a four-lane bridge that spanned the divide.

We had driven our family vehicle over to the airport and left it parked there during our time away, fully expecting to just jump back into it and head home after we landed. But that wasn't to be. Upon arrival at the Mactan airport, we were informed that a cargo ship had been blown loose from its moorings by the typhoon and had crashed into one of the pillars that held up the Cebu-Mactan bridge. We were told that vehicles could be used to get to the bridge entrance, but none were permitted to actually cross the bridge—not even motorcycles. Around 11:00 a.m., in the midst of a regular day of high heat and humidity, and with a fever of about 103 degrees and every muscle screeching, I walked all the way across the bridge alongside Helen and the kids. I literally thought I was going to die.

A few of our church members picked us up when we got to the other side and drove us home. The city had been devastated, with almost every power pole having been blown down. The electricity had already been off since the storm, and it would take seven more days from the time we arrived back home for our power to be back on. No electricity also meant no running water. Flushing toilets and taking showers had to be done by way of buckets of water that we had to carry by hand into the house. By God's grace, a young man who attended our church and lived in our subdivision had an uncle with a well on his property. He blessed us by supplying us with the water we needed to live day by day until things got back to normal.

After a miserable first night back at home with no change in how I was feeling and no electric fans to help keep cool, I went to the ER the very next day. They diagnosed me with typhoid fever and wanted to admit me to the hospital. Instead, I asked them what I needed to do to be able to go home and recover there, and they gave me the instructions and released me. I didn't spread it to anyone and wound up getting better a few days later, and eventually life went back to normal.

Reinvigorated by another miracle

Of all the trials we went through during that season, the most difficult one was ministry related. I had been investing a significant amount of my time into a man that I believed might be capable of eventually stepping into my role as the pastor of the church. But in a completely unexpected turn of events, his company promoted him to a position of increased authority and transferred him to one of their larger offices in a very large city on a huge island in the South. As he shared the details with me, it was clear he really didn't have any other options, and I knew that if I were in his place, I would accept the better position and the transfer too. A few weeks later, we said goodbye to him, his wife, and his beautiful family.

I was absolutely crushed emotionally, and my overactive mind went into overdrive trying to understand why God would permit this to happen. I concluded that this was probably God's way of telling me that it was time to shut things down and move my family back to the States. Surely, if He really was pleased with us, we would have more than the forty or so adults that were attending after three full years of effort. As I shared these thoughts with Helen, we began to pray about whether that was what God was saying, and we decided it would be wise to seek counsel from others missionaries.

Prior to receiving the news about my right-hand man being transferred to another island, I had already planned on taking the boat to Manila to attend a huge pastors' conference and to spend some time with some of the other missionary church planters I knew up there in the North. Now that things had unfolded as they had, I knew that God wanted me to seek counsel from the other brothers that had been doing the same, but for much longer. I met with them while I was there, poured my heart out to them, and asked them what they thought. They gathered around me, placed their hands on my shoulders, and took turns praying for me, our family, and our situation with the church.

When the prayer time finished, we all sat back down, and the missionary who had been there the longest looked me in the eye and said that he believed God wanted us to stay in Cebu and remain faithful. He pointed out that it had been almost two years since our last visit to the States, and we probably weren't seeing things very clearly. He concluded by saying that He believed God would provide a way for us to visit the States and then get back to the work He had so clearly called us to do, that we hadn't yet completed. Although what he said made immediate sense, and I wanted to move forward as if the Lord had spoken through this brother, I couldn't summon the faith necessary to begin the planning required to make a trip of that magnitude actually happen.

By the time I stepped out of the taxi that took me from that meeting back to where I was staying in Quezon City, I crunched the cost of a trip like that in my mind. With the airfare costs for a family of five, rent and utilities for our house during our eleven-week absence, and the significant amount needed to cover immigration fees for the category of visas we were on, I calculated that we would need $8,000. The reality was that on a good month, our financial support left us with about $100 in savings, and we had less than that at the moment. This squeezed the final amount of faith out of me just a few hours after that meeting as I plopped down on the bed in the room where I was staying.

As the sun was beginning to set, I decided to walk down the street to a restaurant that I had spotted earlier in the day. As I sat and ate in the restaurant, my mind jumped back and forth between what I had heard at the meeting a few hours earlier, the time I needed to grab a taxi in the morning to get to the docks, and what I needed to begin doing to plan our transition back to life in America. With the sun down and a slight breeze blowing, I slowed the pace of my walk as I retraced the half mile or so path from the restaurant back to where I was staying.

When I had cautiously navigated the last cross street and stepped back up onto the broken and uneven sidewalk, something happened to me once again that I had never experienced before.

The faith to believe what I had been told earlier that day was inserted into my heart and mind from outside of me by the Holy Spirit Himself. Put as simply as possible, the idea of a visit to the States and a return to Cebu to keep doing what we were originally sent to do was like a beautiful plant that God had placed inside of me earlier that day through the other missionary. But the pool of faith inside of me was completely insufficient to give life to it, nourish it, and sustain it, so it had shriveled and shrunk almost immediately—but it was still somewhere within me.

Now, knowing that I had given it up as dead and having no desire or ability to ask Him to revive it, He took the initiative to pour into me the faith that was needed to not just generate it, but to make it flourish to the degree that my lackluster faith needed to latch on to what He was clearly going to make a reality. I knew immediately that this faith was not something God had found within me; it was something He had given *to* me. In other words, I knew that I contributed nothing to it, and that all I needed to do was take Him at His word and begin thinking and acting as if it was a plan set in stone by the creator of the universe.

I was so full of joy that it felt like I walking on air the rest of the way back to the house where I was staying. When I called Helen before I went to bed that night, I told her I had some big news to tell her, but because calls were so expensive and what I had to say was going to take some time, I told her I would wait until I got home. I drank in God's presence, His word, and the beauty of the sea and the many islands that comprise the Philippines during the twenty-four-hour boat ride back to Cebu City from Manila Bay.

When we were alone after my arrival, I told her what had happened in the order it unfolded. The look on her face prior to me telling her the biggest moment of the trip was surprising to me. She had a half smirk on that felt like she already knew what the big news was going to be before I had the chance to tell her. When I finally described that moment on the sidewalk to her, she smiled as only she can, and revealed that God had spoken to her that night as well and told her the same thing. While He was hitting me with that first-in-my-lifetime infusion of faith, He was also revealing to her that He was sending us back to the States for a break, so we could be refreshed and continue on with life and ministry in the incredible city that had become our home.

The next day, in mid-January of 1991, I called my pastor and told him what God had shown us, and that our plan was to visit the US the last week of March and then return to Cebu the first week of June. He said it was going to take a miracle to get the amount of money we were going to need, but that if we were convinced God would provide, he would do everything within his power to help make it happen. For it to work within the time frame we needed, the tickets had to be purchased by the first week of March—at a cost of almost $5,000.

I included our desire to go back for a visit, and how much it would cost us to do so, in the newsletter I sent out the following week. Our pastor also kept the congregation informed of our desire over the next few weeks, but with less than a week to go before our deadline of March 1, less than $300 had been received for the trip. As much as I hated what I was feeling each time I heard how little had been raised, I seriously began questioning whether the sidewalk event had really been God generated. My faith waned. Helen's never did.

At 5:30 a.m. on the Monday of the week we needed to buy our tickets, the phone rang. I was groggy as I answered, but the excited tone and elevated volume of my pastor's voice as he asked me if I was awake yet jarred my brain into gear. Without waiting for me to answer, he told me that we would definitely be making a visit to the States. I asked him what he meant, and he said that someone had placed a $10,000 check into the offering that morning, along with a note that said it was for our church's missions endeavors and that as much of it as necessary should be used to bring the Jacksons back to the States for a break. I was stunned and speechless, which doesn't happen very often. The ring of the phone and hearing my side of the conversation had woken up Helen. When I repeated my pastor's news to her, she smirked again and silently mouthed something to the effect of "I told you."

Mission accomplished

Five weeks after receiving that call, on the last day of March in 1991, everything in Cebu was in place for our eleven-week absence, and we made our second trip as a family back to the States. The weeks we spent there were restful and refreshing, and we headed back to Cebu City encouraged; and once again able to trust God's ability to show us who the man would be that He was calling to succeed me as the shepherd of that small flock. We didn't know how long that would take, but we were committed to stay as long as necessary.

By the fall of 1992, the education needs of our two oldest children, the health of the church, and the deepening connection with a godly man from the church in Dumaguete City, whom we had met when we lived there, provoked us to begin to seriously consider whether the time was approaching for us to transition the church over and return to the States. This man's calling to be a pastor was clear to me and to the fellow leaders of his church.

We mapped out a plan together, and by the end of 1992, he resigned from his job and made the move to Cebu City with his wife and their beautiful family by his side. Within a few days of their arrival, Helen and I had put together our departure plan and settled on April 23, 1993, as the day we would say goodbye to the place we had called home for more than five years and the group of people who were now woven into the fabric of our lives. Although those final few months were incredibly hectic, they went very well, and it was evident to our family, and everyone else involved, that God was at work in the midst of what was unfolding.

The crescendo of the evidence that He was the ultimate orchestrator of all that unfolded while we lived in Cebu happened on our final morning, just a few hours before we tearfully said goodbye to everyone and boarded the plane for our trip back to California. To truly understand the significance of what took place during breakfast that morning, I need to rewind to an important component of the vision that God had originally given us for going to Cebu in the first place.

Just hours before Jesus was arrested, beaten, and crucified, He gave a final briefing to His most intimate followers. Of the many things He told them, God drove three specific truths into our hearts and minds from John 15:16: First, the reality that although we freely chose to follow Him, our doing so was the result of Him having already chosen us. Second, that like the apostles, He too had appointed us to go and to bear fruit. And third, that the fruit that would be produced through our obedience would remain—it wouldn't die, and in fact, would increase after our departure. During the times that I seriously questioned the level of impact we made while we lived and served there, God used the truths and the promise of lasting fruit contained in that verse to keep me going.

More than six years later, we were spending our last two nights in Cebu at the Baptist General Conference guesthouse on the outskirts of the city. Cooking in the rooms wasn't permitted, so three meals per day were prepared by the guesthouse staff and offered in the common dining area. A retired American couple lived on site as directors of the guesthouse and took their meals with any guests who chose to be there for each meal. Before breakfast each day, the husband or wife would read from a small devotional book that listed a specific verse for the day and a few thoughts about that verse. They would then ask the Lord to bless the meal and the day ahead.

As our family sat down at the table for breakfast on that final morning, I was a bit groggy from not sleeping too well. The magnitude of what would take place in the morning weighed heavily on my thoughts and emotions and forced me to toss and turn most of the night. My mind jumped from whether we were leaving too soon, over to wondering what God would have us do next, and then to how all of us would handle the reverse culture shock that I knew the whole family would inevitably soon experience. And honestly, the Bible verses that composed the vision God had given us originally were nowhere to be found on my brain's radar screen that morning.

Suffice it to say, I was having a hard time concentrating on any one thing that morning when the guest-house director grabbed everyone's attention, opened the devotional booklet to April 23, and began reading. I couldn't believe what I heard. The verse for the day was John 15:16. As soon as he read it, all that was stirring in my mind and emotions completely dissipated. I was overwhelmed and astonished once again. Our amazing God knew we needed to have fresh evidence of His guidance over every facet of our lives, and that's exactly what He gave us that morning.

A few hours after that final breakfast as residents of Cebu, Philippines, we tearfully prayed with the thirty or so members of our church who made the one-hour trip to the airport to send us on our way. I knew at the time that it was a moment I would never forget, and just as I thought, the scene is still vividly alive in my memory. Yet as sorrowful as I felt, I was also rejoicing because I knew God was pleased with the joyful obedience our whole family had demonstrated during our five and a half years spent living there.

The British-owned airline we boarded that morning had recently begun flying direct from Cebu to Hong Kong. There was a twenty-hour layover in Hong Kong prior to our flight to Los Angeles, and the ticket price included a one-night stay in a hotel and vouchers for two meals close to the downtown area of Kowloon. All five of us beamed with excitement and joy when we checked into our very luxurious room at the four-star hotel and walked and shopped on the busy streets of Hong Kong. That twenty-hour layover was unlike any other we had ever experienced, in the best way possible. It was the perfect bridge between life in the Philippines and the restarting of life once again in the United States. In fact, that flight, and that layover, were so special to me that whenever I'm asked what the favorite day of my life has been, that's in the top three.

Writings from the mission field

I journaled regularly and wrote a newsletter every other month for the entire five and half years we lived in Cebu. Each year, I also sent out locally made Christmas cards with handwritten notes to our family members, those who supported us financially, and those who let me know that they were praying for us. By our sixth and final Christmas in the field in December of 1992, the list of people that I desired to write a personal note to had grown to the point that I just didn't have time to write to each and every one of them individually. Up until then, I had pridefully resisted what so many other missionaries I knew had been doing: Xerox copying a year-end family update and inserting it inside the Christmas cards and into the envelopes we placed in the mail. But I knew it was time to eat some humble pie and decided to write a poem with an explanation of why that year's Christmas card was different than what they had received on past Christmases. My poem to them was as follows:

HOKEY CHRISTMAS CARD POEM

A Christmas card list that's under control
provokes real pleasure...still it does take its toll

But a Christmas card list that has grown too long,
is very unnerving and deceptively strong

It can take so much time, even wear out your arm,
like a big black cloud that's poised to do harm

Well that's what I faced as I looked at my list,
"What should I do?" Are you getting my gist?

I know you enjoy that personal touch,
but my list is too long; *it's way too much!*

A personal letter I prefer to write,
inside of each card...and I thought that I might

But a Xerox copy saves time *and my hand,*
And yes, it's impersonal; I do understand

So this whole thing is hokey...what can I say?
But: Have a good Christmas! And forgive me I pray!

God bless you, the Jacksons

I also wrote a number of poems for Helen during our time in the Philippines. Here are a couple of them:

Written on nice stationery from the Philippines:

March 31, 1990

Fair Maiden

Although I search for *words* to explain
My love for you, Helen, it's become very plain

That words can never fully impart,
What I feel for you, babe; they're only a start

So other ways I desire to find
To help you to know that you're on my mind

Sometimes it's flowers, sometimes a card,
Sometimes a poem; it's not that hard

But the days go by, and I give no heed,
To certain things that I know you need

I know that you love to be softly caressed,
Just a touch and a hug make you feel so blessed

Yet I seldom do that, and I don't know why,
But I want you to know, that I do hear your cry

Helen, Fair Maiden, I want you to know,
That my love for you, babe, just continues to grow

I know in my heart you're a gift from above;
I'll never stop trying to show you my love

I love you, babe

Written on a store-purchased Valentine's Day Card in 1992:

Helen

My hope was to really show you again
My love for you, babe, but where to begin?

I could buy you a gift, like a dozen red roses;
I could buy you some shoes, to cover your toeses

I could even buy some new perfume,
Or a box of chocolates for you to consume

I could show you my love by any of those,
But I know that you love it when I tell you in prose

So I sat down to write, to write you a poem,
But my mind was empty; no one was home

The words didn't flow; they just wouldn't rhyme;
I tried and I tried; I spent so much time

But the harder I tried, the harder it got,
My brow became sweaty, my chest became hot!

The point of all this, what I'm trying to say,
Is: I love you babe; Happy Valentine's day!

I gave it the old college try, babe. My thoughts are
filled with you. You are a precious gift from a loving
heavenly Father. I love you Helen. —Me

CHAPTER EIGHT

Founder, Father-in-Law, Grandfather (1993–2002)

Restarting life in America

Our church and its members had gone above and beyond in their efforts to ensure that our transition back to life in America went as smoothly as possible. One of the members had accepted a one-year assignment from his company to work in a different state, and they agreed to pay the lease on his current house for the entire year while he was gone. He and his wife joyfully invited us to stay there while they were gone. When we arrived from the airport that first day back, we walked into a fully furnished house. But that wasn't all. The church members had fully stocked the shelves with all kinds of groceries and the other things necessary for day-to-day living. They even donated a car with a full tank of gas. It was utterly amazing and unlike anything I'd ever heard any other missionary describe when describing their return from the field.

We visited local family first, and then made a two-week drive to see the family members that had moved back to Georgia and Tennessee. About ten weeks after we landed on American soil, I was invited to join the pastoral staff of a local church in San Marcos, just west of where we lived in Escondido. Not long after that, Helen found a part-time position working in the food services department of our local elementary school district. In September, Travis and Jody began attending the local public high school, and Katie started second grade at the elementary school that was less than a quarter mile away from the duplex we were living in.

Reconnecting with a special friend

While we were living in the Philippines, my disabled friend Matt had relocated to the central coast area of California. Not long after our return to Escondido, I called him and discovered that he came to visit our area on a fairly regular basis. Some of the folks from our church that I had connected him with years before had become close friends with him. Their friendship was so deep that even though it required a huge effort on their part, they invited him to visit a few times each year, and they were willing to pick him up at the train station in Oceanside. They would take care of him for however many days he was there and then get him back to the train. Without thinking it through or asking them everything that was involved in taking care of Matt during such visits, I convinced Helen that we should be his hosts for his next trip to Escondido.

By then, both of us had cars, and mine was a small economy car. After spending time with him the first time,

I remembered how difficult it was to lift him out of his chair and get him into the passenger seat, belt him in, and then fold up his chair and load it in the back. That would prove more challenging with the car I was then driving. And although I could have made it work with my car, I asked my dad if I could borrow his full-sized, Chevy pickup truck for Matt's visit, and he was happy to switch with me. That definitely made the whole transportation segment of Matt's visit much easier, but taking care of his bodily needs—something I had never done—was a whole different story.

When I had spoken to him on the phone prior to our first try at hosting him, I asked what I needed to have ready in order for him to spend the night with us. He said he carried everything necessary with him and that he just needed a couple of blankets put on the floor to sleep on. He was emphatic that because of the way his body was contorted, if he wasn't in the bed specially made for him, it was much more comfortable for him and the person caring for him if he just slept on the floor. I told him that the only place in our little house that would work was right in the middle of our living room. He said that would work just fine, and that's where he slept every night that he stayed with us.

Getting him ready for bed the first night he spent with our family is something I'll never forget. I knew it would take me out of my experience and comfort zone in a much greater way than when I took him out for pizza six years prior. But I trusted that he had had more than enough experience directing other first-timers over the years, and there was probably nothing that I could inadvertently do to him that hadn't been done by another well-meaning soul in the past.

We ate dinner with Matt as a family, and my kids were somewhat shocked at my willingness and skills in feeding him. They had a ton of questions for him, and he happily answered them, and he even lobbed questions about life in the Philippines back at them. After the kids were in bed, Helen and I talked with Matt in our living room for a while and then she said goodnight and retired to our bedroom. After talking about the plan for the next day, he said that he was ready to crash too, and guided me through the process of putting him down for the night.

First, he said that I needed to lift him up out of the chair and lay him on the ground on his back. Next, I had to swivel and maneuver his stiff arms and legs as much as possible to peel all of his clothes off. Then, he verbally walked me through the steps of taking off his diaper, removing his external catheter, cleaning the bag, putting on a new one, rediapering him, and finally putting his pajamas on.

He had been lying on his back and I was hunched over him the whole time I prepared him to sleep. As I finally stood upright, I asked if there was anything else I needed to do before I headed to my bedroom for the night. He flashed that sneaky grin that I had seen the first time when I took him out for pizza. He said that the last thing I needed to do was turn him over onto his stomach, which was how he actually slept every night.

Due to the rigidity of his shoulders and upper arms, I told him I had no idea of how to do that and asked him to walk me through it. He told me to move up to where his head was resting, squat down, put a hand under each arm pit, lift his torso up, and then turn him over, trusting that his hips and legs would follow and come to rest in the right spot. I counted aloud to three and then tried to follow his instructions.

But I did something wrong in the process and he began wincing in pain just before he came to rest on his stomach. I had no idea what I had done to him and he could tell I was panicking. A pained grin came to his face and with his teeth gritted, he said that I had dislocated his left shoulder, and it was really painful. He told me to move around to that side of him, put my foot in his armpit, grab his stiffened forearm with both hands and pull outward without moving my foot and press on the top of his ribcage. I did what he told me to do, and his upper arm went back into place in his shoulder socket.

He immediately stopped wincing and looked directly at me and told me I did a great job. He could tell that I was stunned by what had just happened, and as I was about to tell him how sorry I was for what I had just done to him, he got that big old grin again and told me that this happened fairly regularly to him and that quite a few other people had also dislocated his shoulder over the years. I asked him why he didn't warn me ahead of time. He said it would have created too much stress for me. And since knowing about it doesn't always prevent it from happening, he said he kind of enjoyed seeing the way people panicked when they realized what they had done. He then said that pulling a fast one on people like me made the pain a little easier to bear.

What's within me unleashed again

The evening before I needed to take him back to the train station in Oceanside, Matt went out for Italian food with some friends. After they brought him back, I did the evening routine for him and told him I'd wake him and get him ready to roll by 6:00 a.m. He was already awake when I went into the living room that morning, and he said that his stomach wasn't feeling too well. I asked him if he was okay to make the trip ahead, and he said he was. I got him ready, loaded him and his things into my dad's truck, and we left my house right on time.

About fifteen minutes into the thirty-minute drive from Escondido to the Oceanside train station, his stomach was gurgling loud enough that I could hear it, and he started passing extra-pungent gas, the kind that required the windows to be rolled down even though the temperature outside was in the midforties. He apologized immediately after each time he did it and said that he couldn't help himself. I tried to lessen his embarrassment by humorously sharing a few of my own digestive adventures over the years, especially some of the really funny ones when we lived in the Philippines. It seemed to help a little, but it was very obvious that he was still experiencing the stomach issues and his chuckling with me didn't really mask how ashamed he was feeling.

About a half mile from the train station, he sheepishly told me that he couldn't keep things in the realm of gas any longer and needed to fill his diaper. And boy did he. At that point, even with the windows down, it took every fiber of my willpower to act as if it was no big deal.

As I pulled into the driveway of the train station, he told me that there was no way he could ride on the train for six hours in the mess that he was now sitting in, and he humbly asked me to clean him up. I told him I would give it my best shot. I parked, and breathing through my mouth because of the smell, got him situated in his chair. I strapped his suitcase to his lap with a bungee cord in the same way I did when I picked him up, and pushed him to the only place at the train station that would make an undertaking like that possible—the public restrooms. Because this is Southern California, the restrooms were made of block, with concrete floors, and they were open air at the top, under the roof. In other words, there's no climate control, and it was as cold, or colder, inside the restroom as it was outside.

I wheeled him to the side of the doorless stalls, and he told me that the only way I could do what needed to be done was to lay him down on his back on the cold concrete floor. He said to grab some of his dirty clothes from inside his suitcase and lay them on the ground to keep his skin from being in direct contact with the ground.

When I had done that, I picked him up from his chair, and as I was about to lay him down I discovered that the mess released into his diaper had gone all the way up his back and soiled both his shirt and his pants too. My mind immediately flashed back to when my kids had done the same, quite a few times, prior to them being potty trained. But the fact that I had to plunge in and do for a grown man the same thing I had done for them as children required a greater level of just grinning and bearing it than I had ever exerted before.

As I began swiveling him around to peel off his soiled and smelly clothes, a wave of disgust at what I was having to do rose up within me. A previously unknown facet of anger erupted inside me, and I had this powerful urge to lash out in words at Matt for putting the two of us into this horrible, disgusting, and inconvenient situation. A civil war was taking place inside me, and I had to consciously battle a part of me to restrain it from taking control and putting into words the obviously ungodly and selfish thoughts that were now a part of my mind. I remained silent, and as soon I removed his diaper, he began shivering, and then his teeth started chattering as he lay there buck naked on the ground, with only a few shirts between his bare backside and the cold concrete.

Still not saying anything, I began cleaning him up as quickly as possible with the baby wipes he carried with him at all times. While doing so, two guys talking to one another had entered the restroom, and as soon as they rounded the corner to where the stalls were, they came upon us. They stopped in their tracks—speechless and dumbfounded—as they saw one man leaning over another man that was naked, helping him put his clothes on. An even larger wave of embarrassment gushed from deep within me, generated by a fear of how they would interpret what they were seeing. I immediately sensed that I needed to explain what was happening, which I did, along with apologizing for what they were seeing. They told me that it wasn't a problem and that they would come back a little later, and then they walked out.

As soon as they left, my spirit and soul began grieving at what had once again sprung up from within me.

I hated it, and I knew that I needed to process what had just happened as quickly as possible after getting Matt on the train. As I finished getting him dressed and loading all of his things on his wheelchair again, I told him that it had been one of the most unique mornings I'd ever experienced. He said it was for him, as well.

A few minutes later, with his luggage on the train and him seated in his chair on the train's wheelchair lift, he was visibly exhausted, and his eyes were watering as he apologized for all that had just taken place. I told him there was no need for him to do so, and that these are the kinds of things brothers in Jesus do for one another. When the conductor raised the lift and closed the door, I turned around and began the long walk to where I had parked my dad's truck.

When I closed the door, I leaned over the steering wheel and began to cry and shake with an intensity that I had never felt before. What had just taken place had completely unhinged me emotionally. I was appalled at the fact that I unconsciously responded to what was taking place through a grid that had my feelings, my convenience, and my comfort at my highest priority.

I had made the whole situation about myself, rather than the needs of a brother in Jesus whom I deeply loved. I began crying out to God to forgive me for the depth of the self-love that was still within me and the anger and embarrassment that it spawned. After thirty minutes or so, He assured me that His forgiveness was granted, and He let me know that it took something of this magnitude to move me to the next step in the journey of me becoming more and more like Jesus.

Pioneering another church

A few weeks later, I received a call from the Filipino woman that God had used so strategically to direct us to the Philippines. Although we didn't attend the same church, we still stayed in contact with her. She told me that she had some Filipino friends who were interested in hosting a Bible study at their house and that she thought I'd be perfect to start teaching them. It seemed like it could be God driven, so I dived in and began teaching a weekly Bible study at the home of the woman who had requested it. Through a number of interesting circumstances, we all became convinced that God was guiding us to take the steps necessary to become a Filipino American church.

Our first official church service took place in early April of 1994, just less than twelve months after stepping foot back in America. The church eventually became somewhat multiethnic, and within a few years, we were making a significant impact in a variety of ways in our local community. We financially supported missionaries from the outset, and it wasn't long before we began sending some of our own members to the foreign mission field.

One year, two poem-worthy events

In 1996, two significant events took place within our family that provoked me to write more poetry. The first was Travis's high school graduation in June. We had agreed to his plan to move back East with our family in Tennessee a few weeks after he graduated and spend some time working for Helen's dad at the sandwich shop franchise he owned. The transition out of high school and into the next season of his life and the fact that he would be leaving from our influence and under our roof to continue on both weighed heavily on my heart and mind. And although we planned on blessing him with a typical graduation present, I also knew that God wanted me to give him a gift straight from my heart—a poem written specifically to him. So, I wrote him the following:

His will first, Travis

Travis, my son, the time has now come to take the next step in your life
If you seek His will first, that step will bring joy; if not the fruit will be strife

The reason I say this, I want you to know, is because I have seen Him in you,
And if you are His, which I do not doubt, then His will is what you must do

He's given you gifts—I've seen them myself—gifts that when placed in His hands
Will glorify Him, and satisfy you, content that you're part of His plans

So I challenge you, son, to give Him afresh, give Him all that you are today,

And look to Him for the strength that you need, the strength to help you obey

For the world is strong, and the enemy too, eager to see young men fall,
Always trying to stir up your flesh, or get you to question His call

Now I'm confident, Trav, that He is your Lord, that your walk just isn't a show,
But *you* must believe it, *you* need to be sure; it's essential that *you* really know!

And if you desire, which I think that you do, to please Him in all of your ways,
Get into His Word, and take it to heart, and you'll grow the rest of your days

Finally, Trav, I want you to know, the great joy you have brought through the years
I love you, I'll miss you, I'm proud of you, son— there really is joy in these tears!

Ps. 119:9 How can a young man cleanse his way? By taking heed according to your Word

Prov. 23:15 My son, if your heart is wise, my heart will rejoice...

Prov. 23:19 Hear my son, and be wise; And guide your heart in the way

A few months later, we began planning a party for my mom and dad's fortieth wedding anniversary. Their love for each other was obvious to everyone who knew them, and the way they continued to live out their wedding ceremony vows to one another was exceptional. I sensed that God wanted me to acknowledge that with a special poem. Here's what I came up with and read to them at the party we held for them in November of 1996:

Marriage Honored
Mom and Dad's 40th anniversary poem

Commitment is something not common today, something not easily found,
And though that is true, I know it exists; I'm sure that it's still around

And how do I know? I've seen it myself! And believe me that I'm not alone
The family has too, and all of your friends; commitment is what you have shown

You stood before all; you committed yourselves; you vowed it would be for life
The road up ahead you knew would bring joy and occasional seasons of strife

And time has now proven you both were sincere
when you said, "Till death do us part"
Through richer, through poorer, through sickness
and health, nothing has torn you apart

Now what's really a blessing, what's truly unique, is
a love that grows deeper each day,
And that's what we've seen in you, Mom and Dad:
deepening love is what you display

You're so tightly joined; your names go together;
it's hard to think of just one,
They can't just say "Tom"; they can't just say "Bev";
if they do, they know they're not done

They have to complete it; they'll say "Tom and Bev,"
or switch it and say "Bev and Tom"
For Rick and myself, we think "Mom and Dad"; if
not, then it's "Dad and Mom"

So we all join together and speak from our hearts;
we want you to know this is true,
That the way you have loved these last forty years
gives marriage the honor it's due

Founding Shepherd's
Staff Mission Facilitators

In January of 1997, while still pastoring the multiethnic church, I was asked to begin teaching global

missions-related classes at the new campus of the main Bible college within our group of churches. At the same time, an increasing number of former and current missionaries were contacting me to seek counsel about a variety of personal and missions-related issues they were dealing with. Needless to say, with pastoring the church, teaching at the Bible college, trying to be more than just a teacher to my students, and random missionary counseling, I didn't have much down time.

In early 1999, the combination of all I was engaged in began to bring to life some of the visionary thinking I had done just before leaving the Philippines six years earlier. Prior to our departure back to the States in April of 1993, I had made another trip by boat to Manila to personally visit and say goodbye to my many missionary friends I had gotten to know over the years. The topic of where we would be living and what we would be doing upon our return to the States was a part of each conversation. Every time I described where things were at on that front, I always included how we had been sent directly to the mission field by our home church and cared for exceptionally well over the years. I always added that even though I didn't know how they would do it, we were trusting they would be as diligent about expressing their love and care upon our return as they had during our whole time in the field.

This inevitably led them to describe their connection to their home church, the role their missions-sending agency played in their lives, and the interface between them. Every one of these conversations provoked my natural inclination to analyze things and engage my mental gears. The result was envisioning the possibility of creating a hybrid global missions organization that would exist to facilitate the efforts of local churches that desired to send their own members directly to the mission field. With all that went on during those final few months over there, and the first few years back in the States, I was forced to move my thinking about creating that hybrid entity to the storage shelves in the bank of my mind. This is where it sat until I began digging through those shelves again as the year 1999 progressed.

The incredible care we received from our home church while we were in Cebu, and especially the way their showered their love upon us after our return, moved back to the forefront of my mind. By September, I was able to put the vision, mission, and core values of Shepherd's Staff Mission Facilitators to paper and move things forward. I then contacted a few pastors and men from the business world who each had a passion for global missions, shared the vision with them, and asked them to pray to become a part of the board of directors.

As I moved forward to take the administrative steps necessary to create a new global missions organization and began to think about how to let others know about it, a number of completely unexpected situations arose that moved me to postpone the actual start of the ministry by about eighteen months. In the interim, I accepted the executive director role at an existing missions organization and began working with the staff of that entity. Eventually, that relatively short detour from the time frame I desired actually provided some of the key building blocks that became major contributors to the effectiveness of Shepherd's Staff once it was brought to life.

Another poem, becoming a father-in-law and a grandfather

Our oldest daughter, Jody, had graduated from high school in 1997, and at the time, I seriously considered writing a poem for her, as I did for Travis. But as I pondered whether I should, and I concluded that since I would probably end up writing only one poem for each of my children, and both of my daughters had shared some of their excitement and dreams about their wedding day at some point in the future, I decided to wait. Almost three years later, Jody had fallen in love with Michael, a young man in the military. Their relationship deepened, and I had the privilege of doing both their premarriage counseling and then performing their wedding ceremony in November of 2000. Just before the father-daughter dance during the wedding reception, I read this poem that I wrote for her on her special day:

Giving away treasure

As I ponder the things taking place on this day,
my mind is retracing your life
So many great memories race through my mind;
on this day you become Michael's wife

"You know I was thinking" with that funny accent
"Housekeeping" is stuck in my head
"I don't like to sweat," and of course there's my favorite:
"Daddy's going to bed"

When I think of you, Jo, I think of these things,
and I'm touched to the core of my being
My first little girl becoming a bride…
it's hard to believe what I'm seeing,

But it really is true; I must come to grips
with these things that are so hard to swallow
Although I rejoice, and I'm happy for you,
I'm feeling a little bit hollow

To see the young woman you've grown up to be
makes me proud and brings me such pleasure
And honestly, Jo, to give you away
is to let go a part of my treasure

Yet I know that it's right, that God has been good,
that this is a part of His plans
I've seen that Michael loves you more than himself,
and I trust you're in very good hands

And one final thing, you knew it was coming,
that I'd get there sooner or later:
Your marriage and Michael are a gift from the Lord,
our incredibly good Creator

The one you've both sought to pour out His blessings
upon your union this day
is the one you should follow the rest of your lives,
true joy is found in His way

So seek Him first, for He is the key
to your marriage being all that it should
Confess your sin, turn and trust in Him,
for you've tasted that He is good!

Ps 34:8 Oh, taste and see that the LORD is good;
blessed is the man who trusts in Him!

At the time of Jody's wedding, Travis had already graduated from the Bible college where I was teaching and had been serving as a missionary in Belize, Central America. He had been developing a romantic relationship with the daughter of a family we were longtime friends with, and that our church had also sent to serve as missionaries in Belize where Travis was serving. One thing led to another, and in June of 2002, less than a month after Jody and Michael blessed us with our first grandson, Anthony, I had the honor of performing my son's wedding ceremony too. Within a time span of a little more than eighteen months, I had two more identity itches scratched. I was now a father in-law twice over, and a grandfather for the first time.

Stewardship requires a change

Shepherd's Staff had gotten traction fairly quickly, and the numbers of churches and missionaries being served were steadily increasing. By fall of 2002, it had become obvious to me that if I continued to both pastor my church and direct the ministry of Shepherd's Staff, both of them would suffer. Because of the way I'm wired, I also knew that burnout could become a real possibility for me. I was convinced each ministry deserved a dedicated leader that would give it the attention, direction, and care God designed it to have, and it was no longer possible for me to provide that for both.

I sought counsel and prayer from a number of mature men of God, and each of them advised that I needed to view the decision through the lens of stewardship. Specifically, they asked me whether the experiences, knowledge, network, and platforms God had blessed me with were put to better use as the pastor of a local church or the director of an organization that was serving dozens of churches now and probably hundreds in the future. What they told me basically confirmed what Helen had been telling me all along, and confident that God was guiding, a short time later I turned the church over to a missionary friend who also previously served in the Philippines. I was on fire with passion and excitement about the future as I jumped full time into the role of directing Shepherd's Staff Mission Facilitators to become all that God wanted it to be.

Although I initially missed many aspects of pastoring a local church, I loved the challenges and opportunities that directing a global missions organization provided. Meeting with the pastors and leaders of churches, spending quality time getting to know their members God had called to go, and equipping their churches to really nurture them was incredibly exciting and satisfying to me. All of the above, coupled with the opportunities to train prefield missionaries for cross-cultural life and service and the time and freedom to travel internationally to encourage missionaries in the midst of their day-to-day lives, kept me in a constant state of exhilaration and ongoing bewilderment at how God was continually outpouring His grace onto me.

I described my life at the time with a saying that I learned from my dad, the mechanic. My life was like a big-block V-8, with the engine hitting on all the cylinders and running exactly as it was designed to run. I was making an impact for Jesus in a number of ways—on people, churches, and the world—and I was loving every minute of it.

CHAPTER NINE
A "Terminal" Disease Recipient (2002–2004)

A poet keeps writing

I was doing quite a bit of traveling for Shepherd's Staff the first year after I began directing it full time. As had always been the case, Helen was a constant in my thoughts, and I missed her incredibly while completely enjoying what I accomplished on each and every one of those trips. I felt an ongoing need to express my love for her in poetry, and knowing she loved when I did, I wrote a few more poems for her. I wrote this for her one Mother's Day:

> Helen, my love, you're a virtuous wife;
> I'm sure that you know how I feel,
> But you're more than that, babe;
> You're a gift to our children;
> He's used you to show them He's real
>
> From the day they were born
> Till right up to now,

You've selflessly loved them His way
You listen, you care, you show them His love,
Through their mom God has been on display

I haven't expressed,
And neither have they,
As often as we really should,
How thankful we are for your life and your love;
Through you we *know* God is good!

And this one, using the title I bestowed on her not long after we began going steady:

Fairest of Maidens

O fairest of maidens, I've asked our Lord for grace to express anew
In the form of a poem, with words that rhyme, the depth of my love for you

O fairest of maidens, I use the term, since it clearly does reveal
The place in my heart, that's yours alone...expressing just how I feel

O fairest of maidens, your smile brings joy; your touch does soothe my soul
Each day with you, I thank God for, you're His gift that makes me whole

O fairest of maidens, how can it be, that you would be my wife?

That one so fine, so other-focused, with me would
share your life?

O fairest of maidens, I've had a taste, of what God
had in mind
Two lives made one, bound up in Him, a marriage
by His design

O fairest of maidens, with this I close, you're a
precious work of art
Made just for me, by an awesome God, I pray
you've heard my heart

A malfunctioning body,
a variety of tests

Going back to the illustration I referenced earlier about
my life hitting on all eight cylinders, near the end of
2003, the cylinder of my physical body began to misfire.
I began to get severe cramps in muscles that had never
cramped before. My shoulder muscles seized up after I
sneezed. My jaw muscles would lock when I yawned too
widely. My neck muscles froze if I looked to either side
too quickly, or if I just kept looking to the side for more
than a few seconds. Reaching across my body to grab the
shoulder seat belt to buckle myself in made the muscles
in my side cramp up. At the same time, I started twitching
in different parts of my body, including my face. I began
having this feeling of popcorn popping under my skin,
which became more pronounced when I was sitting still

or lying in bed trying to get to sleep. It got to the point where Helen started noticing it in bed whenever we were touching. She could feel the movement going on in my muscles underneath my skin.

Our initial thought was that something was lacking in my diet, so I started taking different supplements, exercising a little more—including riding our recently purchased mountain bikes more regularly—and drinking more water to be sure my body stayed hydrated. None of those things seemed to have helped. And I noticed that increasing the time on the mountain bikes didn't seem to increase the strength in my legs, but on the contrary, it was actually making them feel weaker.

In January of 2004, Shepherd's Staff was conducting a three-week premission field training course in Tijuana, Mexico. This is just over an hour's drive from where we lived in North San Diego County. One of my roles was to take the teachers for the course across the border, where they would spend the day instructing our students, and then drive them back across into the US and get them to where they needed to be. On one particular day, I had taken a good friend, who was a board member and a medical doctor, across the border to teach the students. He did a great job as usual, and we enjoyed the time in the car on our way down and on the way back north.

We were talking about a number of different things while we waited in an incredibly long line of cars slowly inching forward to cross the border back into the United States. As we talked, he noticed that the top part of my cheeks and my chin would twitch every now and then. Eventually, he asked if I could feel that my face was having these twitches, and I told him that I only felt it happening every now and then. He then asked me how my body was doing overall, and I told him about all the unusual symptoms that I had been experiencing over the previous few months. After listening to me describe what had been going on, he didn't probe any further, and the conversation moved on to baseball and our beloved, but frustrating, Padres.

A few weeks later, while I was up north in San Luis Obispo teaching one of the classes of a fifteen-week course on world missions, he paged me, requesting that I call him back when I had a few minutes. When I did, he told me that he had been thinking about what he had observed in my facial muscles while we sat in the border traffic and the symptoms I had described to him. He also said that he had been doing some research, and he was concerned that my symptoms could be the result of a very serious neuromuscular disease. He told me to contact my primary doctor as soon as I returned to Escondido and to request a referral from the doctor to see a neurologist.

By the time the conversation was finished and I hung up the phone, I had a sense that a radical change was on the verge of taking place in my life. Prior to that call, I had been able to pretty much ignore the strange things that my muscles were doing, acting on their own. I thought that it was probably an age thing and a new normal for me that I needed to get used to. But all of that changed as a result of that call. As much as I tried to concentrate on being prepared for the lesson I was scheduled to teach that night, I couldn't keep my mind from running down a path toward a worst-case scenario and what would be produced for Helen and my family if that was the journey I would be embarking on through no choice of my own.

A few days later, my primary doctor examined me, ordered a couple of nerve-related tests, and referred me to a neurologist. He sent me for a number of tests that would determine whether my symptoms were neurological rather than mechanical, and then eventually ordered me a muscle biopsy. This entailed extracting about an inch and a half of muscle from my upper left arm and my left thigh to run tests on them. He had already told us that the results of this test would probably make a definitive diagnosis possible. When his office called me to schedule an appointment to go over the results, Helen and I, and the rest of our family, knew that a significant family event would happen that day.

Engulfed by ALS, surprised by a teenager

The appointment was set for Monday, May 17, 2004. Travis was already married and serving alongside his wife, Liz, as missionaries in Belize, Central America. Jody and Michael were living and working locally, and their son, Anthony, would be celebrating his second birthday a few weeks later. Katie was the only one living at home with us. She was seventeen and just finishing up her senior year of high school. She was part of her high school's chorus and show choir, and they were scheduled to perform at a competition at Disneyland that Monday.

She knew I had an appointment scheduled for that day, but we hadn't told her about its potential significance.

We all felt like it would be better for her to make the trip with her classmates and keep her mind engaged with other things. And since she probably wouldn't be back home until after 6:00 p.m., we thought that if the diagnosis turned out to be bad news, we would have at least a few hours to process the news so she wouldn't have to see us all in the midst of the emotion.

We invited my mom and dad to come along with us to the doctor's office for my 1:30 p.m. appointment. As I opened the door and followed Helen and my parents into the lobby, I was keenly aware of the other two people that were already seated and waiting to be called for their appointments. As the four of us sat down, I nervously tried to talk about other topics, hoping to lessen the weight of a potentially devastating diagnosis. When it was clear it wasn't working, I joined them in their silence. My eyes wandered to the other two patients who were also waiting, and I found myself pondering whether their appointments were going to be as momentous as mine was probably going to be.

Finally, the receptionist told us that the doctor was ready to see us, and we all stood. We hugged my mom and dad, and they sat back down. As we opened the door that led from the lobby toward the examination rooms, my doctor's nurse was there to meet us. I was expecting her to guide us to the room where I had always met with him before, but she didn't. Instead, she walked us right by it and motioned for us to enter into his personal office. At that point, I was 100 percent sure that the news was going to be bad, very bad. And I was right.

When we entered, he immediately stood from his chair and slowly walked out from behind his desk, picked up a folder that was lying near the edge, and motioned for us to sit down in the two chairs that were facing his desk. He took a few steps backward and leaned back on the corner, facing us. He handed us the results of the muscle biopsy and said that he was now certain that I had developed the disease known as ALS, which was more commonly known as Lou Gehrig's disease. He told us how sorry he was for having to give me this diagnosis, and that neurologists dread giving it the most. He spent a few minutes explaining what it was, how it usually progressed, and how important it was going to be for us to be prepared for the end result it would probably produce sometime in the near future.

My doctor friend had already told me that my symptoms could be an indicator of ALS, so I had been doing quite a bit of reading about the disease, and because of what I learned, I had been begging God for the source of my problems to be something other than the one that brought down the great Lou Gehrig. I hadn't passed onto Helen most of what I had discovered because I didn't think there was any reason to give her the details about a terrible disease that I might not even have. When the doctor gave us that life-changing news, it wasn't surprising to us, but it did shock us to our core, and we were overcome with sadness.

My parents stood up as soon as we reentered the lobby, and they could tell by the look on our faces, and by our demeanors, that the news was bad. We hugged in silence there in the lobby. We didn't give them the details until the four of us left the building and walked toward the car. Within an hour or so, Jody and her husband joined the four of us at our house, and as we all stood together in our kitchen, I gave them the details on what the doctor had said, and we explained how everything was going to be very different from then on. We hugged, heaved with sobbing, and probably went through a box of tissues within about a half hour.

Eventually, the heavy sobbing subsided, and through tears, we began talking through what the future could look like if the disease followed the path that it normally did. I can't remember who it was, but someone said that it was a good thing Katie was going to be gone for a few more hours. If she saw all of us in the condition we were in at that moment, she would have been absolutely crushed, which would in turn, crush all of us again. We all nodded in agreement and kept discussing how we were going to navigate the future.

Not ten minutes later, while we were still standing in a makeshift circle in the kitchen talking and crying, we heard the front door open and shut and the sound of Katie's typical fast-paced steps come down the hall toward us in the kitchen. When she turned the corner, she saw her mom and dad, her sister and brother-in-law, and her grandparents turn toward her with red, swollen eyes. This stopped her in her tracks, and she raised her hands with her palms up and asked if everyone was crying because we had just been told Jody was pregnant again.

Before Jody could answer, I stepped toward Katie and told her we had gotten very bad news from the doctor—I had been diagnosed with a terminal disease. She immediately burst into tears, rushed toward me, threw her arms around my neck, and hugged me ferociously while sobbing almost uncontrollably—all of which thrust the rest of us back into sobbing mode. My tears fell all over the top of her head, and her tears soaked the front of my shirt at pocket level.

Just before Helen and everyone else moved in and created a hugging and sobbing huddle, Katie grabbed me by each bicep, extended her arms, leaned back, and looked me right in the eyes. She blurted out that this meant that she needed to get married much sooner than she had planned. I heard what she said, but I didn't understand what she meant, so I asked her what she was talking about. She said that I had to walk her down the aisle on her wedding day, and there was no other option for her, so her wedding would need to take place sooner than she had envisioned to be sure I could do for her on her wedding day what she had always dreamed of.

It probably goes without saying, but I had never thought about what would surface primarily in the heart and mind of a seventeen-year old girl who just discovered that her dad had a terminal illness. But now I knew. And as a father who loves his daughters more than words can describe, the real possibility of not being able to give this daughter what I had been able to give her older sister, and what she so clearly longed for, was another crushing blow to my soul.

The ripple effects of a terminal diagnosis, unwanted identity embraced

The differences in the way Helen and I are wired came to surface within a few weeks of the diagnosis. I wanted to be as prepared as possible for how things would probably unfold, so I spent even more time researching the progression of the disease. To me, the more I knew about what might be ahead and how I could personally prepare for it made it possible for me to help Helen and others know what to expect and how to be prepared themselves. But she didn't see it that way. And the more I tried to tell her what I had learned, the more exposed the differences between us became and eventually morphed into one of the greatest challenges we'd ever faced in the twenty-six years we'd been married.

Knowing her as well as I did, I should have known what her perspective was, but I wasn't paying attention. I was so focused on trying to help her with what I thought would minimize the impact of the progression of my disease on her that I didn't consider what she believed would keep the impact manageable for her. Eventually, we did sit down, and I was able to really listen to what she had to say and then made major adjustments in what I would share with her, when I should, and how I should.

Once the shock of the diagnosis and the surreal first few weeks that followed had passed, I knew it was time for me to scrutinize the convictions I held about suffering. The hours and hours I had spent over the years trying to bring comfort and encouragement to people who were either suffering themselves or suffering as a result of what was happening to their loved ones had contributed to what I referred to as my theology of suffering. Having this clarity on this important and very relevant subject had enabled me to help people. Did I really believe the truths about suffering that I both spoke to others and also operated by? Were they as understandable, reasonable, and biblically based as I thought they were prior to being forced to apply them to myself and my family?

To make a long story short, I concluded that although my convictions about the tension of believing and interacting with a God who was goodness in the essence of His being yet permitted suffering, were solid as far as they went, they didn't go far enough. I still absolutely believed that whatever happened had been permitted by God, and that in some way that we may not currently understand, His glory and worth can be reflected through our response to it. But what was lacking, at least for me, was the transition from trusting in Him to entrusting myself to Him—in other words, intentionally placing every fiber of my being, including the relationships I had with my loved ones, entirely into His hands, and entrusting all of us into His care, and believing that He would empower all of us with the capacity to stand firm in our relationship with Him regardless of what He permitted to unfold.

I ultimately concluded that my understanding of the role of suffering in my own life and those of my family's represented God and the truths of His word sufficiently. So, I followed the advice that many people had given me and contacted the ALS Association of San Diego. Helen and I made a trip down to meet with the leaders. After hearing our story, they asked me if I'd be willing to serve as an unofficial chaplain for the ministry. They said that to accept the role, I needed to be willing to meet with ALS patients that were much further along in the progression of the disease than I was. This meant also possibly meeting with their families in order to help them understand the resources ALS of San Diego had to offer. I accepted their offer and had the opportunity to help a few fellow ALS patients and their loved ones.

When Helen and I walked out of the ALS Association of San Diego's office that day, I realized that my ALS diagnosis had bestowed another new group identity upon me. No one intentionally volunteers to join this group. I certainly didn't. What bonded us together as a recognizable group was being diagnosed with an illness that a very small minority of people suffer from. But it wasn't just the diagnoses that we shared; it was the similar progression of symptoms, the futility generated by receiving treatment that could only relieve the symptoms—not cure the disease—and the unique emotional trauma that we as patients and our families began experiencing when the diagnosis was given. And it was not only the fact that we would die much sooner than any of us ever imagined; it was also the understanding that the journey toward the end would likely include both a progressive inability to communicate and a transition into complete dependence on others to provide us what was needed to sustain our lives. I was at the point in my relationship with God and my family that I was able to not only accept, but embrace having an identity as an ALS patient, while also understanding why the vast majority of people are swallowed up with discouragement and depression when they discover they have acquired it.

Although my mind was consumed with health and family affairs during the first few weeks after the diagnosis, I also knew that some major decisions needed to be made regarding the ongoing and future ministry of Shepherd's Staff. By the first week of September in 2004, the decision was made to move the ministry to Albuquerque, New Mexico. A former elder in my church, who was a good friend and whose wife worked for the ministry, was willing to give up his lucrative career, relocate, and step in as my successor. The woman who managed the administrative side of the ministry spoke with her husband, and he was also willing to make the move. So, with a small group of people fully committed to doing what was best for the ministry, Shepherd's Staff's administrative office relocated there in early 2005.

The other major issue that Helen and I felt strongly about settling as soon as possible after the diagnosis was where we should be living if the disease progressed as quickly as it was sometimes known to do. We decided to put our condo up for sale and move to Mesquite, Nevada. The first and foremost decision behind this was the fact that my older brother (who, as aforementioned, was married to Helen's older sister) had just relocated there after serving in Belize, Central America, for the previous six years. The four of us have always had a special bond with each other for obvious reasons. Even more importantly, they both had the experience and the heart to walk with us down the path that we would most likely be on in the not-too-distant future.

But the move also made sense for a couple of other reasons, not the least of which was the incredible amount of equity we had in our condo, as the whole country was experiencing a housing boom at the time. Although the housing prices in Mesquite were increasing, like they were all over the country, the prices in San Diego were outpacing them. We knew that the profit we could make by selling our condo would give us a huge down payment on a much bigger house that would cost about half of the price ours would sell for. And not only that; we'd have enough to remodel it the way we wanted and to make the changes necessary for it to be wheelchair friendly. Those two factors, along with the plan our son had to move back to Mesquite in the middle of 2005, had clinched the decision for us.

A surprise birthday party interrupted

With the decision to sell our place and make the move to Mesquite behind us and my forty-sixth birthday approaching on September 14, just a few weeks away, I couldn't keep myself from thinking about how many more birthdays I might have left. We went to my parents' house for dinner on the thirteenth, which was a Monday night. After dinner, I felt a type of nausea that I had never experienced before but didn't really give it much thought. Around eight thirty, I told Helen and my mom that I wasn't feeling too well and that I was ready to head home. By the time we had walked out to the car, I told Helen that it would probably be better if she drove home because I was feeling worse by the minute.

As we made the right turn out of the mobile home complex where my parents lived and onto one of the main streets in Escondido for the drive home, I had sudden, supersharp pains that shot up my right arm, and then I felt pressure in my chest. I started sweating profusely and laid my seat back, and Helen asked me if I was okay. Then it felt like someone dropped a fifty-pound anvil on the center of my chest, and through clenched teeth, I told her that I thought I was having a heart attack and that she should head straight for the hospital, which was about two miles further down the road we were already on. She increased her speed but had to back off when a light at the upcoming intersection changed to red as we approached. The pain in my chest increased, and I told her to look around, and if it was safe, to run the red lights to get me to the hospital as quickly as possible.

Less than five minutes and three ignored stop lights later, she screeched up to the emergency room doors at the hospital and jumped out of the car. That entrance had already been locked for the night, but a security guard was sitting on the other side of the glass doors keeping an eye on things. When he saw this woman in such a panic run around the front of the car and open the door for me, he stood up and walked toward the locked doors. Then he saw me try to get out of the car with Helen trying to help me. I looked at him and pointed to my chest with a terrified look on my face, and he understood immediately what was going on. He ran to the doors and hit the open button, ran back inside to call for an ER nurse, and then came back out to help us. With Helen under one arm and the security guy under the other, we had just gotten through the doorway, when a nurse and another ER worker met us with a gurney, and some nitro tablets were placed directly under my tongue before I was even lying down on it.

The nitro stopped the pain almost immediately, and I began to calm as they ran an EKG and a slew of other tests. About three or four hours later, a cardiologist placed a stent into my artery known as "the widow maker." The damage to my heart was very minimal, thanks to a number of factors, not the least of which was Helen's ability to stay calm while driving as fast as possible with her husband in the seat next to her clutching his chest and most likely worrying that he might not make it long enough to celebrate his birthday a few hours later.

I did wind up spending my birthday in the hospital recovering, but I was released the following day. The outpouring of love I received from my family and friends was off the charts. I was already on the hearts, minds, and prayers of most of them because of the ALS diagnosis, but the heart attack provided a specific moment and opportunity for them to tell me how much they loved and appreciated me. But what I didn't know at the time was that most of them were already planning to show their love and appreciation for me at a previously scheduled surprise party that really caught me by surprise.

It had been scheduled for the Friday after my birthday, but because of what had just happened to me, everyone decided to push it back a week. They lured me to the party by saying that Helen and I had been invited to a missions meeting that was being held in the fellowship hall of a large church in a nearby city. Some very close friends worked at the church, and they had already visited me in the hospital, and so had the pastor of the church. When invited to a missions-related meeting at the church, when it was already ten days past my birthday, I completely believed that was what it was. Boy was

I wrong. They totally pulled a fast one on me, and it was very cool.

There were probably close to two hundred people in attendance, and they put together an incredible program. They set it up with the intention of wanting me to hear and know at that moment how they all felt about me—saying publicly what they loved and appreciated about me, rather than waiting to say it at my memorial service. It was amazing. It was powerful. It was possibly the greatest gift I've ever been given by the people that I knew and loved up to that point in my life. They had even arranged for Travis to come back up from Belize and surprise me in the midst of the party. It was unforgettable.

CHAPTER TEN

Refugee Advocate
(2006–2012)

Transition, horizon extension discovered

With the heart attack, my actual birthday, and the crazy birthday party/prememorial service in our rearview mirror, the plan to make the move to Mesquite really began moving forward. Even though we would be relocating to almost four hundred miles away from our family in the Escondido area, and the separation would be brutal, everyone agreed that the move was the wisest option available. We began preparing our condo for sale, and Helen's sister began keeping an eye out for just the right house in Mesquite. In early October, she found a four-bedroom, single-level house that also had an office and a pool. It was just around the corner from the house she and my brother had recently purchased. Our condo sold very quickly, and we bought the house Helen's sister had found. In mid-November, we made the move to Mesquite.

Once we were fairly well settled, in early 2005, I contacted ALS of Nevada in Las Vegas to find out the services they offered and to see if I might be able to help them. After connecting with them by phone, we made the eighty-mile drive into Vegas to meet with them face to face. When they heard my story, they not only asked me if I'd be willing to do what the San Diego branch had asked me to do; they also asked if I'd be willing to be a spokesman for them at different informational and fundraising events. I told them I was happy to do so, and I wound up helping them a few different times.

In early 2006, they asked us if we would be willing to be their representatives at the ALS Association's national convention that was scheduled to be held in Washington, DC, that year. We agreed to go, and they took care of all of the expenses for us to attend. We learned much more about the disease, the research being done to find a cure, and the amazing array of services being provided by the various associations around the country. Because of the Lou Gehrig connection with the disease, most of their gatherings included at least a few current or former Major League Baseball players. For a total baseball geek like me, this ramification of the disease was a welcome flicker of light in the midst of seemingly endless darkness. Tommy John, the Dodgers pitcher who had been the recipient of a specialized surgery done on his pitching arm was at the conference, and I was able to meet him and get a picture taken with him.

After our return from the trip for ALS of Nevada, I discovered that I had developed type-2 diabetes. This meant that I was going to need to start taking a couple of pills each day and it prompted some major changes in my diet. As 2006 continued to unfold, we noticed that the speed with which my symptoms had been progressing appeared to be slowing down. I still had the same issues, but they hadn't gotten any worse, and few of the other symptoms that normally accompany the progression of ALS didn't seem to be present.

That summer, ALS of Nevada told me they wanted to help establish an ALS clinic in Las Vegas. What that means is that they try to get a local neurologist that is familiar with ALS to host a one-day-per-month clinic that brings together the different medical specialists that an ALS patient would need to fight the progression of the disease. They asked me if I would be willing to meet with the neurologist that had volunteered to host the clinic and then be a spokesman for its promotion once it began operating.

In August, I once again made the drive into Vegas, this time to talk with, and be examined by, this very well-known and respected neurologist. When he walked into the examination room where I was sitting, I was surprised because he looked like he wasn't even thirty years old. He asked me to tell him my story, and he listened very intently, asking me questions along the way and jotting down notes on a yellow legal pad as I spoke. After about twenty minutes, he put the notepad and pencil down and said he'd like to examine me.

He did the usual muscle strength tests that I had become accustomed to, checked out my tongue, had me do the standing and balancing tests, and then again asked me a few of the questions he'd already asked, this time with dates as accurate as possible. When he finished, he took a step back, leaned back on the counter attached to the wall behind him, and said that it was very possible that I had been misdiagnosed. I couldn't believe what I thought I just heard him say, so I asked him to repeat it. He did, and then added this time that it was obvious I was suffering from a neuromuscular disease, but he was fairly well convinced that it wasn't ALS. He said it was probably a different disease known as Kennedy's disease (which was named after the doctor who originally discovered and described it). He also said that if it was Kennedy's, that it might have been the cause of the type-2 diabetes I had developed because that was one of the effects it produced.

When he saw my jaw drop open, my eyebrows raise, and a completely stunned silence come over me, he told me a few more things about the disease that he believed I actually had. After, he said that there was a DNA-level blood test that could be done that would show conclusively whether I actually had the disease that he thought I had, and not ALS. He also said that before officially recommending that I order the very expensive test, he wanted to do the very uncomfortable needle test needed, known as an EMG, that I had done three times before. I agreed, and a few weeks later, I was back in his office, letting him jab needles into what felt like every muscle in my body—including directly into my tongue. After more than an hour of using me as a human pin cushion, he finally put the needles down and said that I should get that test done, even though he was 90 percent sure I had Kennedy's disease, and not ALS.

Since our move to Mesquite, the only medical care I was receiving was through the VA, so he wrote a note to the VA neurologist I had recently seen and requested that the VA pay for the expensive test to be done. My VA neurologist agreed and filed the request, and it was approved. A few weeks later, my blood was drawn and sent to the Mayo Clinic in Minnesota. The results were sent to my VA neurologist a few weeks after that, and with Helen at my side for the appointment with him the third week of September of 2006, he told us that the test showed that I did have Kennedy's disease, and not Lou Gehrig's.

Under any other circumstances, if you were told by a doctor that the muscle issues you're experiencing are the result of a neuromuscular disease and are likely to cause you to lose the ability to speak or swallow and possibly even to walk within the next fifteen to twenty years, it would be devastating news. But when you've already been told you have ALS and you've been preparing yourself for a horrible journey that will likely cause you to die in less than five years, the Kennedy's disease diagnosis can produce unspeakable joy and an excitement about a future that you were convinced you would never have—like a life horizon that has been extended. And once again, my identity was broadened through no choice of my own into the group of people that had the Kennedy's disease diagnosis as the tether of their unity.

The valley of the sun, becoming an advocate for refugees

We didn't want to tell most of our family members and friends about a possible misdiagnosis until we knew for sure that was the case. But once it was confirmed, we put the word out to everyone, knowing that literally thousands of people, in countries around the world, had been praying for us since the ALS diagnosis was given almost two and a half years before. We were flooded with people telling us through various means how thankful they were for God answering their many prayers to spare my life. Many of them were convinced God had healed me, which wasn't my perspective (because that would mean the definition of healing would need to be broadened to include going from one terrible disease to a bit lesser of a terrible disease). But whatever their perspective was on what we had been through, we rejoiced with them and thanked God wholeheartedly that I didn't have ALS.

One of the first calls I made was to a good friend of mine who pastored a very large church in Las Vegas, whom I had known since our time living and serving in Cebu. When he heard the news, he asked me to join the staff of his church and retool their in-house school of missions and to oversee the numerous people from around the world that were part of the church, many of whom I met in different ethnic gatherings that took place throughout the week. I went onboard in early October of 2006, and by mid-April of 2007, Helen and I were sensing that the time was drawing near for us to make another move and enter into the next season of our lives and ministry that He had prepared for us.

Even though we didn't know at the time what that next step would be, in May of 2007, I told my friend who had become my boss during the previous eight months that I would be leaving. He had graciously given me the opportunity to teach the Wednesday-night Bible study for the previous six months. My final day as a staff member concluded that evening with me unpacking the final verses of a chapter from the Gospel of John on the last Wednesday of June. On Friday, I was contacted by another brother in the Lord that I came to know not long after starting Shepherd's Staff. He was living in the Phoenix area and knew my background as a missionary, and also that I had done ministry in refugee camps in Thailand quite a few times over the years. He had also taken a few trips over there to help in different ways and had maintained contact with an American missionary familiar with the people of one of the ethnic groups that were living in the different camps. She let him know that quite a few of the refugees she had come to know had been given the opportunity to start a new life in the United States.

At some point in 2006, the US government made the decision to begin accepting and resettling thousands of United Nations officially registered refugees from Myanmar who had been living in camps in Thailand. Phoenix was one of a dozen or so cities that a few of the government approved resettlement agencies operated in, and by the middle of 2007, about three hundred refugees per month were being given a new start at life in Phoenix. A large majority of one of the ethnic groups, the Karen (pronounced Kuh-Rin), were Christians who had been served by the missionary we knew over there. When they were somewhat settled in Phoenix, they were able to find a local church near them and were given permission to begin holding their church services in that church's building.

My friend in Phoenix had gotten to know some of the leaders of the Karen church that had been established there, and he had told them about my background and that I wasn't living too far away. Two of them had been part of the pastoral training I had done in the biggest camp in Thailand in 2003, and they actually remembered me. They asked my friend to ask me if I'd be willing to go to Phoenix and preach at their church's service on a Sunday morning in July. I accepted the invitation, and less than two weeks after my last day at the church in Las Vegas, I was at a church in Phoenix teaching about one hundred Karen refugees from Myanmar who were living in the United States by way of Thailand.

The church that hosted them had been started forty years before and was still being pastored by the incredible man that God had used to launch it. For a variety of reasons, the number of attendees had dwindled down to about a dozen senior citizens. The pastor and those remaining members had the passion, and the time, to serve their community. When these refugees, who were brothers and sisters in Jesus, were placed into the apartment complexes in the neighborhood surrounding the church, they eagerly engaged with and began helping them in a number of ways. This included offering their building as a place for them to hold their own church services in accordance with their culture and in their own language.

I arrived early that Sunday morning in July, and the American pastor gave me a big hug and told me how glad he was to see me. He asked if I would like to preach at the English service that morning too, and I told him it would an honor to do so. Both services went well, despite the fact that my skills in speaking with a translator hadn't been used in a couple of years. After the services I went out to lunch with the American pastor and my friend from Phoenix. The pastor told us his amazing life story, and he was riveted as I told him mine. As we said good-bye, he told me he would love to see me again soon, and I told him I'd love to come back and do it again, as well.

A month later, I accepted another invitation to teach the two services and made the drive back to Phoenix once again. Helen was with me this time, and after the services, we had lunch with the pastor and his wife. During that conversation, he told me that he had been praying for a younger man to succeed him as the pastor, and prefera-bly, someone who had some experience in dealing with people from other countries, languages, and cultures. He asked me if I had any interest in the possibility of moving to Phoenix, and if so, would I be willing to pray about whether I might be God's answer to his prayers for a successor? It was another one of those surreal moments, and both Helen and I sensed that this church's need, and our availability to meet it, could very well be what He had planned for us to do next.

We did pray, made a few more trips, and became convinced that we needed to make the move to Phoenix. I knew this move would be a huge challenge for Helen emotionally. Although we'd only had a small portion of time with our kids nearby during our thirty-eight months spent living in Mesquite, having her sister, my brother, and their kids and grandkids living in that small town made the time without our own kids nearby bearable.

Moving to Phoenix required us to be completely separated from our own kids, our grandkids, and other family members.

This was going to be the first time we'd been in that position since we lived in Japan while she was pregnant with Travis thirty years earlier. With these things weighing heavily on my heart, I decided to write another poem for her that acknowledged her willingness to stay by my side as we ventured forward for the Lord once again. Here's the poem I wrote to try to encourage her in December of 2007:

Another bend in our path

It's very clear that you love our Lord; it's obvious in so many ways
To share them all would take much too long; it could take till the end of my days!

So in this poem, I'll focus on one; I've seen it again and again
It's no surprise to those that know, who have kept up with where we have been

From life in Japan, to the Lone Star state, and back to the place of your birth,
Then on to Cebu for more than five years, in motion because of His worth

And just at the time when things seemed stable, with a condo to call our own,

Along came the news that rocked our world and
forced us afresh to His throne

We heard once again that we should move, to a
small town known as Mesquite,
To enjoy what was left of our time together, our
lives laid down at His feet

And right at the time when we were at peace, at rest
in His hands till the end,
He lengthened the path we're walking together, a
path with at least one more bend

This bend in our path leads to Phoenix, where the
need is certainly great
Together we'll love by the grace He provides, those
who've been victims of hate

A culture connoisseur's dream

We ended up renting our house to my brother and her
sister and made the move into a small apartment in
Phoenix at the end of December in 2007. The transition
to my leadership of the church began in the middle of
January, and by the end of March, I was in the driver's
seat as the senior pastor of a small Baptist church that
was hosting a refugee church with a congregation more
than ten times as large.

It didn't take long for me to get to know every member of the small congregation, along with the leaders

of the refugee church who were able to speak English. Through the ministry trips I had taken to both Thailand and Nepal, I had some experience with refugees who lived in camps in countries that didn't really want them there. But I had no knowledge at all of what refugees experienced when a country was willing to give them an opportunity to start a new life in its midst. In order to learn as much as I could about what it was like, I not only talked to a variety of refugees, but also met with the senior leaders of the three major refugee resettlement agencies that operated in Phoenix.

Years before, I had begun viewing myself as sort of a connoisseur of culture. This was the result of my conviction that God's written word reveals that diverse languages, ethnicities, and cultures were His original design for humanity prior to creation. His plan from eternity was for people to exist in diverse groups with each of them having their own unique honor, glory, and capacity to reflect His awesomeness in a distinct way. When representatives from those diverse groups unify together to love, serve, and worship Him as He designed them to, they will find satisfaction and fulfillment, and He will be glorified. This is why I believe that He commanded His followers to go and preach the Good News and make disciples from among every one of those groups. I'm convinced that the more I seek to know, understand, and appreciate others' languages, ethnicities, and cultures, the more meaningful my relationship with both the Lord and others will be.

As I got to know the leaders and workers of the resettlement agencies, and they got to know me, one of them asked me to create two classes for newly arrived refugees. One was an introduction to American culture in general, and the other was on parenting in the United States. Eventually, I got to know all of the major players in the world of refugee services in Phoenix, and I even had the privilege and pleasure of serving on two State of Arizona Refugee Resettlement Commission task forces: one for refugee healthcare and the other for refugee employment. By the end of October of 2007, Helen and I had found a good rhythm and a great balance between our time with each other and the multifaceted ministry that we were doing.

Health hits just keep on coming

We had some close friends with young children who had moved to Phoenix to help us with many of the things we were involved in. On Halloween night in 2008, we went with them to a Halloween alternative festival at a fairly large local church not far from where we lived. I wasn't feeling too well by the time we went home and continued to feel worse after we sat down to relax. I decided to go to bed, and about an hour later, I started having some of the same symptoms I had experienced when I had the heart attack in 2004. They continued to worsen, so I told Helen we needed to head for the ER at the hospital that was only a half mile from the apartment complex we lived in. So once again, Helen calmly and safely drove me to a hospital while I was in the midst of what was another minor heart attack.

It turned out to be a different clog in the same artery that had already been stented. They had to add another stent to get things flowing once again. This time, even with having the stent inserted, I was released from the hospital less than twenty-four hours after I arrived. At that point, I'd had enough with the heart issues, so I decided to seek advice from my doctor friend and read a few books in the next few days about how to keep your heart healthy. A week later, I decided to go on a full-blown vegan diet to see if I could minimize or avoid having any further heart problems. I knew that there was no way that Helen was going to join me, but she was more than willing to help me stay on it and to try to avoid eating things in my presence that she knew I would be tempted to devour. I stayed on that full vegan diet for eleven months, but due to the genes I'd inherited, my blood tests showed just a minimal difference in my cholesterol levels. I decided it wasn't worth it and returned to being a carnivore, but with much tighter restraints on myself.

A kidney catastrophe and hiccups from hell

Other than the diabetes and the very slow progression of the Kennedy's disease, I stayed physically well from November of 2008 through January of 2010. Near the end of that month, my dad was scheduled to have a pretty major surgery, and we decided it would be helpful for me to be there. I decided to fly rather than make the long drive, and Katie, who was living with my mom and dad while she was in an apprenticeship program for hair styling, picked me up at the airport. I went to bed early the night I arrived because I needed to be up at 4:00 a.m. to drive my parents to the hospital for my dad's surgery. As soon as I started to drift off to sleep, I felt a strange sensation in my lower back. Having experienced the pain of a kidney stone about twelve years prior, I knew it wasn't that, even though it was in the same basic area. I kept trying to ignore it, but it continued and increased into a weird kind of pain as the hours went by.

I climbed out of bed at 4:00 a.m. and got dressed, and even though I was ready to drive my parents, whatever was going on had gotten worse and spread out all over the lower right side of my back. I finally decided something serious might be happening, so I gave my doctor friend a call, expecting that I'd be waking him up, but trusting that our friendship was at the level that he'd be angry with me if I didn't call him any time I really needed his help. He answered on the third ring and sounded totally alert. He said he was in Washington, DC, for a conference, so he'd been up for a few hours. I told him what was happening, and he said to go to the ER as soon as possible, as something could be seriously wrong.

I was still receiving medical care from the VA, which meant that the ER I needed to visit was a thirty-minute drive away. I was in too quirky of a condition to try to drive it myself, so after I told my mom and dad what was happening, and that they would need to drive themselves for surgery, I woke Katie from a dead sleep and told her I needed her to drive me to the VA hospital ER over in La Jolla. Ten minutes later, she was driving me to a hospital twenty-five miles away at the same time my mom was driving my dad to a surgery center a few miles from their house.

The pain continued to intensify on the drive, and by the time we arrived, it was pretty severe. I could barely stand up straight, as I explained to them what I was feeling. After an injection of some amazing pain medicine, they took me to a room and ran some blood tests and scans on me, and I finally fell asleep. When I awoke, my daughters were both there by my bedside, and the pain had mostly subsided. A doctor arrived a short time later and said they had found the problem. For some totally unexplainable reason, I had developed a blood clot that went to one of the arteries that supplied blood to one of my kidneys. The clot had stopped the blood flow long enough to actually kill the tissue that made up the lower quarter of that kidney.

Needless to say, they had to explain that to me in a couple of different ways for me to really understand what had happened to me. I asked what the cause was, and they said they had no idea, that it was something they had never seen before. Apparently blood clots in veins are fairly common, and blood clots in arteries are very rare. None of the twenty-five or so doctors that came in to talk with me and examine me over the next couple of days had ever heard about or seen what had happened to me before. One of them said that what I'd experienced was an incident worthy of a medical journal. They gradually began decreasing my pain medicine and then put me on blood thinners because they had no idea if there were other clots or what might have produced the clot that took out a portion of one of my kidneys.

I was feeling much better the morning of the second day in the hospital, but right after breakfast, I got the hiccups. And they didn't stop. None of the little tricks I had learned over the years helped. By early afternoon, I asked the nurse if they had anything to stop hiccups. They gave me a medicine, and of course, it didn't work. I hiccupped all through dinner, through the evening, and even while I was trying to sleep. I was miserable. By the next morning, my chest muscles were sore, and so was my throat. No home remedy that any friends or nurses told me made any difference, and believe me, I tried all of them. They kept giving me the medicine as often as they could, but it continued to be of no help at all.

I still had the nonstop hiccups when they released me after three nights and sent me away with a supply of a self-injection blood thinner and orders to see my primary doctor at the Phoenix VA the following week. By the time I left, the kidney pain was a thing of the past, but the hiccups were still inflicting pain on me and annoying my loved ones. As hard as I tried to hiccup silently, I just couldn't do it.

Helen had driven over to San Diego that first day I was admitted to the hospital, so she drove me back to my parents' house after I was released. We decided to make the drive back to Phoenix the next day, so I had the afternoon and evening to try to rest while still having to hiccup every thirty seconds or so. By the time we loaded up the car to head home the next morning, the time between hiccups was increasing, and six hours later when we pulled in to our apartment complex late that afternoon, the hiccups were gone. The first time I went ten minutes without having to hiccup, I felt like throwing my hands up and dancing for joy.

We scheduled an appointment for me to meet with my primary doctor at the end of the following week, and I stepped back into the routine that I had developed prior to the kidney-killing trip I had unknowingly embarked on almost a week before. The day before my scheduled appointment, Helen dropped me off at the church, where I was scheduled to meet with a young Karen man and train him on some of the maintenance and yardwork that he had volunteered to help us with. As I was moving around, I started having a different kind of pain in the same area of my lower back. But this time, it was much sharper, more along the lines of kidney stone pain. I sat down for a few minutes, praying and hoping that what I feared wasn't actually happening.

Helen had made a quick trip up to the store after dropping me off and had planned on coming back and doing some cleaning while I trained the young man. From where I was sitting, I could see her as she pulled back into the church parking lot, so I stood up and began walking toward her holding my lower back. When she saw me, she stopped the car and jumped out and asked me what was wrong, and I told her what was happening. She told me to get in the car and that she was taking me directly to the ER at the Phoenix VA. And once again, as my wife was driving me to an ER, the pain I had gotten into the car with increased significantly. It now felt like someone had taken a six-inch-wide ax and jammed it into the right side of my lower back, and they were pushing it in deeper and deeper. By the time we arrived, I could barely stand up and had a hard time thinking about anything but the excruciating pain I was experiencing.

I was given an injection of that heavy-duty pain medicine, had a bunch of tests run again, and was placed into a room in the hospital. The scans they ran showed that the source of my pain was dead tissue from the part of my kidney that had died being passed through the remaining good part and then trying to pass through the very small tube by which the liquid from the kidneys passes. They said there was nothing that could be done to fix it, other than trying to control the pain produced as the tissues went through. They didn't know how long it would take to clear it all out, but that it would eventually. Knowing that first afternoon in the hospital what was actually going on provided a certain level of emotional peace. Not knowing how long I'd be there until things were back to normal then became the primary stress producer, at least for me.

After finishing dinner that first night in the hospital, I was feeling no pain at all and was eager to just crash and get some good, pain-free sleep for at least a few hours. But just as Helen kissed me goodbye to head back to our apartment, I started to hiccup. Helen paused in her tracks and turned around. As she looked into my eyes, her sadness for me was evident. Thirty seconds later, I hiccuped again. By then she was standing next to me, holding my hand in both of hers. She then told me how heartbroken she was to see me have to deal with this issue once again. I couldn't believe this was happening. The possibility that I had been swallowed up once again by what I had begun calling the hiccups from hell generated frustration and anger inside me. Five minutes and ten hiccups later, I knew that I needed to accept the fact this was probably going to be my reality for at least the next few days, but hopefully not forever.

I ended up spending six nights in the hospital that time. When it was certain all of the tissue had passed, I got my release orders. But I still had the hiccups. And just like my time in the VA hospital in San Diego, no medicine or other traditional remedy stopped them. They had lasted three days longer than the previous case I had, and the soreness in my chest and throat muscles reminded me of that fact every thirty seconds or so.

I was still hiccupping on the afternoon that I was released, so I went on the internet to see what I could discover. I really didn't think there was a connection between blood clots, kidney problems, and hiccups, but I decided to look at that possibility anyway. And sure enough, there wasn't. Then I started researching the medicines they had been giving me, and that proved to be a dead end too.

Just about the time I was ready to give up, I came across an article that said opium-based medicine and painkillers cause the diaphragm of a small percentage of people to spasm, which is basically what produces hiccups. As soon as I read that, I knew that was the problem. I had been administered opium-based painkillers both times, and after the first time, the hiccups finally went away about twenty-four hours after the last painkiller I took. I decided right then and there that I wasn't taking another one of the morphine pills they had sent me home with. Six straight days of hiccups was enough. By the middle of the next day, I was hiccup free.

A buckled knee and a bladder malfunction

In late April of 2010, about six weeks after I had been released from the hospital, I parked my car in the church lot, jumped out and closed my door, and took a step toward the entrance to the church with my left foot. When my foot hit the ground, my knee buckled quite a bit, and I almost fell forward onto my face. I didn't feel too much pain in my knee at that moment, so I kept walking toward the church to do what I needed to do. But as I walked around, my knee pain started to increase, and it started to feel a bit swollen. I finished what I was doing a few minutes later and gimped out to my car, surprised at how painful and swollen my knee was becoming.

When I got home, I threw some ice in a plastic bag, wrapped it in a towel, lay down on the couch with some pillows under my leg, and put the ice right on top of it. Helen got home from cleaning someone's house about an hour later, and by then, the pain was even worse, and my knee had swollen to the size of a small cantaloupe. If I moved it at all, the constant pain I was having increased. Now if you've been reading up to this point, you know what happened next. Helen drove me, once again, to the ER at the VA to have my knee examined.

I explained to them what was going on with my knee at that moment, along with the fact that I had major surgery done on the knee when I was twenty years old. I had to have a large pin inserted into it to repair the damage done while I was playing football at a local park with my family. Besides asking what had happened to me, they also asked about my health history and what medicines I was currently taking. I had just finished telling them when an orderly arrived to wheel me over to the radiology department.

He pushed me back to the room in the ER where Helen was waiting, and about an hour later, a doctor came in. He said that when my knee buckled, it tore some of the soft tissue and possibly even scar tissue that was left from the surgery all those years before. Apparently, that happens on a fairly regular basis to quite a few people as they get older. He went on to tell us that the problem with my knee was the result of the blood thinner I had been taking over the past ten weeks. When the tissue tore, the blood was too thin, and it gushed out inside and around my knee. If I wasn't on the blood thinner, it would simply be a matter of putting a syringe-type needle into my knee, draining the blood, and then staying off the knee while it healed.

He told us that wasn't an option because of how thin my blood was due to the medicine I was on. Not only that, he said that if I stopped taking the blood thinner in order to drain the blood out of my knee, it would take at least a week for it to thicken up. That wasn't a viable option because a possible consequence of letting my blood thicken could be the development of another blood clot that could be even more dangerous than the one that took out a part of my kidney. He told me to just keep my knee elevated and iced, and eventually the pool of blood would be absorbed, and I would be back to normal. He offered to give me an opium-based pain reliever, but I told him about my hiccup issue, so he prescribed non-opium-based pain pills.

I wound up having to lie flat on my back with my leg up for about a week, and then spending yet another night in the hospital when it looked like it had gotten infected. It was back to the couch for another ten days or so before the swelling and pain had decreased enough for me to begin navigating with a wheelchair and crutches. During that time, I actually needed to use a wheelchair to help me fulfill a commitment I had made to speak at a missions conference and a church in the Philadelphia area in May. Many of the people that I'm still in contact with from that area still remind me about the time they heard me teach a few sermons from a wheelchair.

After all of the physical health issues that had come upon me during the first half of 2010, I was literally thanking God for each week and month that passed with nothing new happening. After the third straight month of no issues, we were hoping the coast was clear for a long, long time. But it wasn't. At the beginning of September, I began experiencing urinary-related issues, which included a couple of different kinds of pain. Without going into unnecessary detail, through a process of excluding what could be causing my symptoms, the urologist told me that the source of my problem was probably bladder related. He said that looking inside my bladder with a microscope and grabbing a piece of it for a biopsy was the only way to really determine what the cause of my symptoms was. He also said that discovering a form of cancer in my bladder was a possibility that I needed to be prepared for.

As a result of all that we had been through over the previous six years, there was very little news about my physical issues that provoked genuine surprise in Helen. So, giving her the news that there was a possibility of me having cancer didn't totally rock her or my world like it probably would have done to most people. In fact, our mindset was that with all that God had permitted to come upon us thus far and how He had strengthened us for walking through it all, why wouldn't He let cancer become part of our story too? As we talked it through and prayed about it, we decided to not tell any other family members, including our kids, about the bladder inspection I was scheduled to undergo.

Of all the medical tests that I've had done over the years, that was by far the most awkward and embarrassing, which sort of ruined the fact that it really wasn't painful. The urologist let me watch what he was doing on a video screen and described what he, me, and everyone else in the room was seeing inside of my bladder. Everything looked normal. He took a piece to test it just in case and then gently pulled the camera out from inside my bladder and back out through the same undescribed channel he used to enter it in the first place.

We went back a few days later for the results, and they were negative for cancer. I was still having the issues, though. He said the only thing left to consider was that my bladder was having nearly nonstop spasms, and that men don't usually have that issue, but that it may be related to the neuromuscular disease I had. He told me that he was only speculating, but it may have been my bladder getting cramps on a regular basis that were similar to the muscle cramps that had become a part of my day-to-day life. He said there were three different types of medicine that stopped bladder spasms in three different ways and that he wanted to give that a try. He was clear that it would be a process of elimination and sent me home with one of the types of medicine. Within a few days of taking that medicine, the pain and the issues I was having diminished, and I was back to normal.

A miracle for refugees

In early January of 2010, just a few weeks before I took the trip to San Diego to accompany my dad to the hospital but actually wound up being hospitalized with the kidney problem myself, a radical idea that I was convinced was from God had been stopped in its tracks. The brainstorm I had was to turn approximately two undeveloped acres of property that the church owned into an organic community garden that could be used to train a dozen or so refugees on how to farm and hopefully generate extra income for them. I knew that one of the refugee resettlement agencies had a program to do just that kind of thing and initiated a meeting with the key person who oversaw that arm of their organization.

When he heard about the size of the land I was talking about, and our willingness to possibly enter into a lease for them to use it for less than one hundred dollars per year, he was very interested in exploring the idea. After walking the property and asking questions, he said that if it was possible for us to ensure that agricultural water could be supplied for the irrigation of the land, rather than the water that came from the city's supply, they would be more than happy to begin putting a plan together to make it a reality. With that information in mind, I called the company that supplied agricultural water and asked them if their pipes ran close to our property.

The company sent one of their guys out to inspect our land and their nearby connections. After checking everything out, he said they could supply the water for us, but we would need to pay the approximately $70,000 cost necessary to add a connection point for our property to their existing pipe structure. At that point, I concluded my idea obviously wasn't God's idea and then focused my attention on the trip I was about to make to help my mom and dad.

I never gave the project another thought as my crazy health issues unfolded over the next month and a half. But on the fifth day of my six-day stay at the VA hospital due to the kidney tissue problems, and with my hiccups still going strong, I received a call on my cell phone from the agricultural water supply company. The man introduced himself as a representative of a department in the company and said they loved the idea that generated our inquiry about the connection and that they had discovered a way to provide the connection *at no cost* to the church! He told me that the only way they could do this for us was if we agreed to permit them to begin the work by the end of that month.

I had successfully kept my hiccups undetected from him up to that point in the conversation, but as soon as I heard him say those words, my attempt to express my thanks was immediately interrupted by a hiccup that I knew he heard. I apologized to him and said that I was suffering from a hiccup attack that I had no control over. It was a little awkward to actually tell him that, but it was true. I hiccupped through our discussion about the details that needed to be in place for them to start the work and then ended the conversation. I was so pumped that I couldn't keep myself from offering hiccup-influenced praise and thanks to the Lord for His goodness.

More than a few people over the years had told me that getting a favorable decision for a project from a public utility takes an act of God. And those I had previously told about what the utility had originally said to me used the same terminology. But it turned out that God did act, and the project began moving forward.

With the water supply connected, the city required a six-foot block wall around the whole area, rather than the eight-foot chain-link fence we had planned to erect. The cost for that was exactly $30,000. But with every costly requirement the city placed before us to complete the project, God supplied the funds we needed through a variety of sources. Some came from a church in Albuquerque, some from the large Rotary club that met at the Phoenix Country Club, and some from Christian businessmen who loved the positive impact the project would have on some of the most vulnerable people in our local community.

It took months to finish everything necessary to prepare it all for the first planting, including some intensive training for the twelve refugee families that would become our first batch of farmers. We held a huge ribbon-cutting and grand-opening ceremony with representatives from the Rotary, leaders and workers from the sponsoring resettlement agency, the retired pastor of our church, and almost every one of our members. I prayed publicly, giving thanks to God for how He provided all that was necessary to make that day possible, and then committed all of it into His hands for His glory and the good of others. As of October of 2020, the garden is still in use and is blessing both refugees and the people of Phoenix.

CHAPTER ELEVEN

Returnee, Resource (2012–2020)

Life coming full circle

The last few months of the year 2010 passed without any further physical challenges coming upon me. That trend continued, as did life and ministry throughout 2011. But during that period of good health for me, other than the diabetes and the Kennedy's, my dad's health problems increased in frequency and variety. By September of 2011, Helen and I began to think and pray about the possibility of moving back to Escondido to be able to help my mom and dad deal with the ever-increasing health issues he was experiencing that were consuming their day-to-day lives. As much as we loved the members of our church family there and the meaningful relationships we'd developed with so many people in Phoenix, we concluded that the Lord wanted us to begin putting everything in place to make the move back before the summer of 2012.

I had never completely disconnected from Shepherd's Staff, talking fairly regularly with the executive director over the years and helping out as much as I could with the time I had available. I kept him informed of what we were planning, and when it was clear that things were moving forward, he asked me if I wanted to begin doing some part-time work again for the ministry as soon as possible. I sensed this was another demonstration of God's grace and care for us and happily accepted the offer.

As the transition away from the church in Phoenix unfolded over the first few months of 2012, he spoke with the board of Shepherd's Staff about the idea of having me step back into full-time work for the ministry as the director of church relations and missionary care. They loved the idea and approved it unanimously. Within a few weeks of our move back to the Escondido area, on Memorial Day weekend, I began working full-time once again for Shepherd's Staff.

We moved into a condo a few streets over from where our oldest daughter and her family were living in San Marcos, the city just west of Escondido. It was the first place we had looked at when we had made the trip over to find a new home a few months prior. The owner was a widow, and she met us there and showed us around. We had a great conversation about a variety of interests that we shared, and we agreed to rent it right then and there. We never looked at anything else. We knew this was where He wanted us to be for the next season He had for us, so we pulled the trigger. Although it was a little further away from my parents' than I originally envisioned being, we could make the twelve-mile drive to the mobile home park where they lived on the east side of Escondido in about twenty minutes.

As Helen and I were eating dinner a few weeks after we had settled into our new house, we talked about the number of life-trajectory-changing things that God had permitted to unfold as a result of the ALS diagnosis. We were convinced that the ripple effects produced as a result of what eventually turned out to be a mistaken diagnosis had shaped us into the people we were at that moment—with the exact life inventory that He designed us to have for what He wanted us to be doing right then, and for whatever came next. The more we talked, the more we recognized that God had moved us into a season in which He was bringing a few facets of our lives, relationships, and experiences full circle.

Helen, the granny-nanny

While we lived in Phoenix, Helen had done an incredible job of supplementing our income through cleaning houses. She's exceptionally gracious, kind, and meticulous in everything she does. But she's off the chart when it comes to intensity and thoroughness in cleaning houses. The first older woman's house she cleaned was so impressed with her as a person, and as the best house cleaner she'd ever hired, that she began spreading the word and telling her friends. Within a few months, Helen had more than enough jobs to keep her far busier than she had originally planned. Even though they all understood the reasons for us making the move back to California, they were absolutely crushed when she gave them the news.

As awesome as she is at housecleaning and connecting with those she worked for, the intensity of the way she cleaned had started to take its toll on different parts of her body. Due to our knowledge of the cost of living in the area we were moving back to, we knew that she would need to generate some more income to supplement what I was making. We really didn't want to have her go back to housecleaning, and in a conversation prior to actually making the move, Jody, our oldest daughter, talked to her about watching her three kids. Since we would be living less than a mile away from them, it was as convenient as it could possibly be. They needed the tax benefits provided by paying for childcare, so they were happy to pay Helen to watch her own grandkids—and she was overwhelmed with joy at the opportunity to do it. When we told our friends, many of whom were also grandparents, I told them I was married to a granny-nanny. And like us, they were thankful that God had orchestrated things so that this amazing wife, mom, and grandmother would be paid to do what she absolutely loved.

Back on board with Shepherd's Staff

When I came back on board full time with Shepherd's Staff, the ministry was serving more than one hundred different churches and almost two hundred of their missionaries who were serving in more than fifty different countries. Although the majority of the churches being served were from the group of churches that I had always been a part of, the numbers of denominational, associ-ational, and independent churches were increasing. The executive director had fine-tuned the administrative sys-tems, and the office staff were gracious and incredibly efficient. The ministry that I reengaged with was larger, healthier, and more impactful at a significant scale than it was when I had been forced to resign because of the ALS diagnosis, seven years prior. It also had more than enough capacity for continued numerical growth, and its future was exciting.

After getting up to speed on many facets of the min-istry that my time away had removed the need for me to know about, I began putting meat on the bones of a posi-tion in the organization that hadn't previously existed. I loved the fact that people much more competent than I was were managing the administration of financial resources, technology, and corporation- and IRS-related issues. With those areas covered, I was free to concentrate on and operate within a realm that I loved, had the most experience in, and had genuine vision for.

I was also given a budget for ministry-related travel, along with the freedom to take as much time as necessary to do so. I've been able to meet with leaders of churches we served around the country and to train or teach at quite a few of them, and I have had the freedom to accept opportunities to teach at both missions conferences and pastors' conferences. And joy of joys, I've also been able to travel internationally. Most of those trips have been for care and encouragement of the missionaries Shepherd's Staff serves, and some have been opportunities to teach at various conferences and retreats (which always includes expressing love for and encouraging those that attend, many of whom are missionaries).

A daughter's dream fulfilled

When we moved into the condo in San Marcos, just a few blocks away from Jody and Michael and their kids, Travis and Liz and their two kids were living in Mesquite. Katie Joy, our youngest daughter, was still single, sharing an apartment with a girlfriend she'd known since high school and working as a master stylist at the salon where she had done her apprenticeship. She had dated a few guys over the years but hadn't yet met a man that she believed was of marriage quality. And we all thanked God that my corrected diagnosis relieved her from what probably would have been her own self-generated pressure to find a husband quicker than she would have preferred.

About a year after our return to the area and through a number of interesting circumstances, she began dating a very solid young man named Blake. As Helen and I got to know him, we both concluded that he was composed of husband-quality material, and he was clearly in love with our daughter. Katie didn't hold the same view initially, but as time passed, she fell for him too. With our approval, he asked for her hand in marriage, and a wedding date was scheduled. I had done some pastoral premarriage counseling with Jody and Michael, and also Travis and Liz, prior to performing their wedding ceremonies, and I did the same with Katie and Blake.

I knew it was now time for me to write a poem for her, just like I did for Travis at his high school graduation, and Jody on her wedding day. As my poetic juices began to flow, I knew that none of our immediate family were likely to have forgotten what Katie blurted out in the kitchen the day I received the ALS diagnosis. Helen and I sure didn't. In fact, we were overwhelmed with thankfulness to God for hearing the cry of our daughter's heart and now graciously giving her what was so obviously important to her. With that thought enveloping all of the other memories of her life that I had percolating in my mind, I began writing. This is what I read to her in front of everyone gathered at her wedding reception in June of 2014:

Sharing a special gift

I thought the dream had come from God, a dream like none before,
Another GIFT from our gracious Lord—that's what He had in store

So I told your mom about the dream; she rolled her eyes and smiled
With Travis and Jody both in school, did we want another child?

So we talked and prayed, and prayed and talked, and decided to move ahead,
Convinced that we had heard from Him, that we'd heard just what He said

I thought this child, this GIFT from God, would surely be a boy,
But if I was wrong and we had a girl, we'd name her Katie Joy

As we all know, I was mistaken; I'd only been half right
You've been a GIFT from our awesome God; you've brought such joy and light

When you were little, in Cebu, you were called a "walking doll,"
And thanks to Trav we all found out, you could cling onto a wall!

You've been my spud, you've been my strudel, you've been my Kitty Kot,
And you looked so cute in your tracksuit, but a track star you were not

You always were a girlie girl, you cared how everyone dressed
Now as a stylist, you've earned respect; to your clients you're the best

We've asked our Lord since you were little, to bless you with a man
Who would love you more than life itself and be your biggest fan

He's heard our prayer; we know it's true; there's
clearly no mistake
Again, God's shown His love for you; He's GIFTED
you with Blake

But that's not all: ten years have passed since we
faced our greatest trial
This day itself is another GIFT…I've walked you
down the aisle

You now have chosen to join your lives—together
in one story
Don't ever forget why marriage exists—to reflect
God's awesome glory

So my heart is joyful, even while it's heavy, but
God's given me a lift
He's let me know what it's like to share a special GIFT

A family history in poem

Since their wedding, Katie and Blake have blessed us
with two more grandchildren, and unless something
very radical happens, it looks like we'll top out with
seven all together. Helen added Katie's two children to
her granny-nanny duties, and in 2016 we relocated back
to Escondido. We were keenly aware that it was another
example of God bringing us full circle, this time back to
the very city where we met and have spent the bulk of
our married life.

In the spring of 2017, we decided to go on a cruise to Alaska with some very close friends to celebrate our fortieth wedding anniversary. As the date of our anniversary approached, I was thinking, once again, about the interesting story we've been living since we met. The more I thought about it, the more I became convinced that God wanted me to write it as a condensed history of our family—something that would not only bless Helen, but that our kids and grandkids would have to value through the passage of time.

But that wasn't all. I also sensed that it should be something that could be put to music at some point in the future. Even though I've always thought I could write lyrics for songs if I put my mind to it, this was the first time that I felt the compulsion to write with a secondary goal in mind. Because of this, I wrote a chorus that succinctly summarizes my belief as to how we've not only stayed together, but have thrived as a family after all these years. As you'll see, I use it as a separator between the key transitions we've encountered on our journey together. You will easily recognize the order and the events I reference in the poem if you've been reading this book from the beginning. Here it is:

His grace has been the key

We knew the odds were stacked against us, those forty years ago
Two naive teens becoming one, convinced our love would grow

Three days later we were in Japan, the learning curve was steep
It wasn't easy, that's for sure, but our love and bond grew deep

Chorus

Growing old together was what we said we'd do
We thought our love was strong enough; we knew we'd make it through
But in His perfect time, He helped us both to see
That for every second since we met, His grace has been the key

When Trav was born, the news was grim, and we boarded that med-evac flight
From Japan to Korea, then to Clark, where we faced our first dark night

We were given beds on the psych ward, then summoned and given warning
His platelet count had continued to drop; he might not make the morning

As we walked up to that incubator, our hearts were filled with fear
Then we gazed upon our newborn son, and hoped that God would hear

So we prayed the way that we were taught; our faith was much too small

Then the chaplain came with holy water and
baptized Travis Paul

Chorus

God heard our prayer and healed our son, and our
life began again
We were sent to San Antonio, where He gave us
Jody Lynn

I was discharged and we headed home, a young
family of four
A normal life was what we wanted, but He had
plans for more

We both worked, and I went to school, and we
developed our routines
We didn't know God was at work, but He was...
behind the scenes

Then He began to seek us out and show us His
great worth
You were the first to receive His love and the gift of
the new birth

He guided us to a local church, and His people
helped us grow
By the time He gave us Katie Joy, He had shown us
we must go

A few days after her first birthday, we boarded Korean Air
And crossed the Pacific one more time, His love and truth to share

Chorus

More than five years later, we left Cebu; the church was in good hands
I was sure that within a year, we would leave for other lands

But He had things here for us to do, and we didn't know the half
He moved us to plant another church and then start Shepherd's Staff

When Travis and Jody finished school, they departed from our nest
We entrusted them into His hands, and His Spirit gave us rest

A few years later, they both were married, and the grandkid phase began
Yet between Anthony and the others came that crushing three-year span

The doctors said it was ALS, that our whole lives would change
But God graced us with a depth of peace that some considered strange

We thought and prayed and then sold our house and
moved up to Mesquite
Two years passed and more tests were run, and the
results were oh so sweet

Chorus

We learned that I had Kennedy's disease; it wasn't
ALS
The invite came to move to Phoenix; we prayed,
then answered YES!

So one more time you willingly went, outside your
comfort zone
You accepted change to do His will and make His
glory known

For the first time since Trav was born, all our kids
were far away
By loving us through our church family, He gave us
strength to stay

A little more than four years later, we moved back
once again
We both knew this was our last stop and gave
thanks for where we've been

Katie got married two years later, both girls were
now wives

Blake now joined, like Michael and Liz, the fabric
of our lives

Anthony, Kristen, JT, Izzy, Lauren, and Lyla too
With Jackson added we're now fifteen; to Him all
praise is due

Chorus

Through a number of God-orchestrated circumstances, in early 2020, a gifted songwriter and sister in
the Lord from the Philadelphia area put it to music in the
exact folk style that I envisioned for it. During Helen's
sixtieth birthday, which we celebrated just a few months
ago, I surprised her with the woman's recording of the
song version of the poem I had written for our fortieth
anniversary in July of 2017.

The full-circle season continues

Although we're thankful for all the new people we've
come to know and love since our return to the Escondido
area, we've had the added blessing of coming back full
circle into face-to-face relationships with many of the
folks we knew years ago. And just recently, after I accepted
an offer to help a Filipino church in the San Diego area
make a transition to a new pastor, it occurred to me
that God had gifted me once again with another part
of my life coming full circle. This opportunity to know,
love, and lead people from a country and ethnicity that

occupies such a special place in our hearts is the latest demonstration of God's incredible grace and goodness in our lives.

Final reflections

Whether it's the people and ministry I'm currently involved with in my local community or globally through Shepherd's Staff, the past few years have been a beautiful and humbling gift from God. He has provided many opportunities and platforms to draw from the inventory of my life experiences that have contributed to making me who I am, enabling me to pass on my understanding of the true and living God's design for identity. I don't know how much more time He's given me to come to the end of my life horizon or what will compose however many seasons are left, but I do know that I plan on using whatever He permits to take place as wisely as possible, pointing the gaze of other people toward the God who created and loves them more than they'll ever be able to comprehend.

ACKNOWLEDGMENTS

Lord Jesus, thanks for calling me out of the darkness and into your marvelous light. Helen, you've been the most tangible expression of God's love for me since the moment He brought you into my sight all those years ago. Thank you for being faithful to the marriage vows you committed to all those years ago. Kristen, thanks for using your blossoming skills in photography to capture my picture for the back cover. To the rest of the family (too numerous to mention individually), thanks for the love you've expressed to us, the compassion you've shown during the many seasons of challenges, and your encouragement to put my life story into a book. I'd also like to share my gratitude to those who helped me in specific ways to complete this task that I've been working on since 2004: Ron, Dion, Debbie, Steve, Jim and Shonda, and Gary and Meef.

For more information, other resources, or booking Jeff as a speaker on a variety of topics, see his website: ThatJeffJackson.com